The Engineers and the Price System

The Socialist Economics of Karl Marx and His Followers

The Engineers and the Price System

The Socialist Economics of Karl Marx and His Followers

Thorstein Veblen

ORIGAMI BOOKS

Published by Origami Books Pte. Ltd.

Origami Books First Edition

Book and cover design by Origami Books

ISBN: 978-981-14-2000-9

origamibooks.co

Contents

The Engineers and
the Price System

I

On the Nature and Uses of Sabotage

"Sabotage" is a derivative of "sabot," which is French for a wooden shoe. It means going slow, with a dragging, clumsy movement, such as that manner of footgear may be expected to bring on. So it has come to describe any manœuvre of slowing-down, inefficiency, bungling, obstruction. In American usage the word is very often taken to mean forcible obstruction, destructive tactics, industrial frightfulness, incendiarism and high explosives, although that is plainly not its first meaning nor its common meaning. Nor is that its ordinary meaning as the word is used among those who have advocated a recourse to sabotage as a means of enforcing an argument about wages or the conditions of work. The ordinary meaning of the word is better defined by an expression which has latterly come into use among the I. W. W.,[1] "conscientious withdrawal of efficiency"—although that phrase does not cover all that is rightly to be included under this technical term.

The sinister meaning which is often attached to the word in American usage, as denoting violence and disorder, appears to be due to the fact that the American usage has been shaped chiefly by persons and newspapers who have aimed to discredit the use

---

[1] Industrial Workers of the World

of sabotage by organized workmen, and who have therefore laid stress on its less amiable manifestations. This is unfortunate. It lessens the usefulness of the word by making it a means of denunciation rather than of understanding. No doubt violent obstruction has had its share in the strategy of sabotage as carried on by disaffected workmen, as well as in the similar tactics of rival business concerns. It comes into the case as one method of sabotage, though by no means the most usual or the most effective; but it is so spectacular and shocking a method that it has drawn undue attention to itself. Yet such deliberate violence is, no doubt, a relatively minor fact in the case, as compared with that deliberate malingering, confusion, and misdirection of work that makes up the bulk of what the expert practitioners would recognize as legitimate sabotage.

The word first came into use among the organized French workmen, the members of certain *syndicats*, to describe their tactics of passive resistance, and it has continued to be associated with the strategy of these French workmen, who are known as syndicalists, and with their like-minded running-mates in other countries. But the tactics of these syndicalists, and their use of sabotage, do not differ, except in detail, from the tactics of other workmen elsewhere, or from the similar tactics of friction, obstruction, and delay habitually employed, from time to time, by both employees and employers to enforce an argument about wages and prices. Therefore, in the course of a quarter-century past, the word has quite unavoidably taken on a general meaning in common speech, and has been extended to cover all such peaceable or surreptitious manœuvres of delay, obstruction, friction, and defeat, whether employed by the workmen to enforce their claims, or by the employers to defeat their employees, or by competitive business concerns to get the better of their business rivals or to secure their own advantage.

Such manœuvres of restriction, delay, and hindrance have a large share in the ordinary conduct of business; but it is only lately that this ordinary line of business strategy has come to be recognized as being substantially of the same nature as the ordinary tactics of the syndicalists. So that it has not been usual until the last few years to speak of manœuvres of this kind as sabotage when they are employed by employers and their business concerns. But all this strategy of delay, restriction, hindrance, and defeat is manifestly of the same character, and should conveniently be called by the same name, whether it is carried on by business men or by workmen; so that it is no longer unusual now to find workmen speaking of "capitalistic sabotage" as freely as the employers and the newspapers speak of syndicalist sabotage. As the word is now used, and as it is properly used, it describes a certain system of industrial strategy or management, whether it is employed by one or another. What it describes is a resort to peaceable or surreptitious restriction, delay, withdrawal, or obstruction.

Sabotage commonly works within the law, although it may often be within the letter rather than the spirit of the law. It is used to secure some special advantage or preference, usually of a businesslike sort. It commonly has to do with something in the nature of a vested right, which one or another of the parties in the case aims to secure or defend, or to defeat or diminish; some preferential right or special advantage in respect of income or privilege, something in the way of a vested interest. Workmen have resorted to such measures to secure improved conditions of work, or increased wages, or shorter hours, or to maintain their habitual standards, to all of which they have claimed to have some sort of a vested right. Any strike is of the nature of sabotage, of course. Indeed, a strike is a typical species of sabotage. That strikes have not been spoken of as sabotage is due to the accidental fact that strikes were in use before this word came into use. So also, of course, a lockout is another typical species of sabotage. That the lockout is employed by the employers against the employees does not change the fact that it is a means of defending a vested right by delay, withdrawal, defeat, and obstruction of the work to be done. Lockouts have not usually been spoken of as sabotage, for the same reason that holds true in the case of strikes. All the while it has been recognized that strikes and lockouts are of identically the same character.

All this does not imply that there is anything discreditable or immoral about this habitual use of strikes and lockouts. They are part of the ordinary conduct of industry under the existing system, and necessarily so. So long as the system remains unchanged these measures are a necessary and legitimate part of it. By virtue of his ownership the owner-employer has a vested right to do as he will with his own property, to deal or not to deal with any person that offers, to withhold or withdraw any part or all of his industrial equipment and natural resources from active use for the time being, to run on half time or to shut down his plant and to lock out all those persons for whom he has no present use on his own premises. There is no question that the lockout is altogether a legitimate manœuvre. It may even be meritorious, and it is frequently considered to be meritorious when its use helps to maintain sound conditions in business—that is to say profitable conditions—as frequently happens. Such is the view of the substantial citizens. So also is the strike legitimate, so long as it keeps within the law; and it may at times even be meritorious, at least in the eyes of the strikers. It is to be admitted quite broadly that both of these typical species of sabotage are altogether fair and honest in principle, although it does not therefore follow that every strike or every lockout is necessarily fair and honest in its working-out. That is in some degree a question of special circumstances.

Sabotage, accordingly, is not to be condemned out of hand, simply as such. There are many measures of policy and management both in private business and in public administration which are unmistakably of the nature of sabotage and which are not only considered to be excusable, but are deliberately sanctioned by statute and common law and by the public conscience. Many such measures are quite of the essence of the case under the established system of law and order, price and business, and are faithfully believed to be indispensable to the common good. It should not be difficult to show that the common welfare in any community which is organized on the price system cannot be maintained without a salutary use of sabotage—that is to say, such habitual recourse to delay and obstruction of industry and such restriction of output as will maintain prices at a reasonably profitable level and so guard against business depression. Indeed, it is precisely considerations of this nature that are now engaging the best attention of officials and business men in their endeavors to tide over a threatening depression in American business and a consequent season of hardship for all those persons whose main dependence is free income from investments.

Without some salutary restraint in the way of sabotage on the productive use of the available industrial plant and workmen, it is altogether unlikely that prices could be maintained at a reasonably profitable figure for any appreciable time. A businesslike control of the rate and volume of output is indispensable for keeping up a profitable market, and a profitable market is the first and unremitting condition of prosperity in any community whose industry is owned and managed by business men. And the ways and means of this necessary control of the output of industry are always and necessarily something in the nature of sabotage—something in the way of retardation, restriction, withdrawal, unemployment of plant and workmen—whereby production is kept short of productive capacity.

The mechanical industry of the new order is inordinately productive. So the rate and volume of output have to be regulated with a view to what the traffic will bear—that is to say, what will yield the largest net return in terms of price to the business men who manage the country's industrial system. Otherwise there will be "overproduction," business depression, and consequent hard times all around. Overproduction means production in excess of what the market will carry off at a sufficiently profitable price. So it appears that the continued prosperity of the country from day to day hangs on a "conscientious withdrawal of efficiency" by the business men who control the country's industrial output. They control it all for their own use, of course, and their own use means always a profitable price.

In any community that is organized on the price system, with investment and business enterprise, habitual unemployment of the available industrial plant and workmen, in whole or in part, appears to be the indispensable condition without which tolerable conditions of life cannot be maintained. That is to say, in no such community can the industrial system be allowed to work at full capacity for any appreciable interval of time, on pain of business stagnation and consequent privation for all classes and conditions of men. The requirements of profitable business will not tolerate it. So the rate and volume of output must be adjusted to the needs of the market, not to the working capacity of the available resources, equipment and man power, nor to the community's need of consumable goods. Therefore there must always be a certain variable margin of unemployment of plant and man power. Rate and volume of output can, of course, not be adjusted by exceeding the productive capacity of the industrial system. So it has to be regulated by keeping short of maximum production by more or less as the condition of the market may require. It is always a question of more or less unemployment of plant and man power, and a shrewd moderation in the unemployment of these available resources, a "conscientious withdrawal of efficiency," therefore, is the beginning of wisdom in all sound workday business enterprise that has to do with industry.

All this is matter of course, and notorious. But it is not a topic on which one prefers to dwell. Writers and speakers who dilate on the meritorious exploits of the nation's business men will not commonly allude to this voluminous running administration of sabotage, this conscientious withdrawal of efficiency, that goes into their ordinary day's work. One prefers to dwell on those exceptional, sporadic, and spectacular episodes in business where business men have now and again successfully gone out of the safe and sane highway of conservative business enterprise that is hedged about with a conscientious withdrawal of efficiency, and have endeavored to regulate the output by increasing the productive capacity of the industrial system at one point or another.

But after all, such habitual recourse to peaceable or surreptitious measures of restraint, delay, and obstruction in the ordinary businesslike management of industry is too widely known and too well approved to call for much exposition or illustration. Yet, as one capital illustration of the scope and force of such businesslike withdrawal of efficiency, it may be in place to recall that all the civilized nations are just now undergoing an experiment in businesslike sabotage on an unexampled scale and carried out with unexampled effrontery. All these nations that have come through the war, whether as belligerents or as neutrals, have come into a state of more or less pronounced distress, due to a scarcity of the common necessaries of life; and this distress falls, of course, chiefly on the common sort, who have at the same time borne the chief burden of the war which has brought them to this state of distress.

The common man has won the war and lost his livelihood. This need not be said by way of praise or blame. As it stands it is, broadly, an objective statement of fact, which may need some slight qualification, such as broad statements of fact will commonly need. All these nations that have come through the war, and more particularly the common run of their populations, are very much in need of all sorts of supplies for daily use, both for immediate consumption and for productive use. So much so that the prevailing state of distress rises in many places to an altogether unwholesome pitch of privation, for want of the necessary food, clothing, shelter, and fuel. Yet in all these countries the staple industries are slowing down. There is an ever increasing withdrawal of efficiency. The industrial plant is increasingly running idle or half idle, running increasingly short of its productive capacity. Workmen are being laid off and an increasing number of those workmen who have been serving in the armies are going idle for want of work, at the same time that the troops which are no longer needed in the service are being demobilized as slowly as popular sentiment will tolerate, apparently for fear that the number of unemployed workmen in the country may presently increase to such proportions as to bring on a catastrophe. And all the while all these peoples are in great need of all sorts of goods and services which these idle plants and idle workmen are fit to produce. But for reasons of business expediency it is impossible to let these idle plants and idle workmen go to work—that is to say for reasons of insufficient profit to the business men interested, or in other words, for the reasons of insufficient income to the vested interests which control the staple industries and so regulate the output of product. The traffic will not bear so large a production of goods as the community needs for current consumption, because it is considered doubtful whether so large a supply could be sold at prices that would yield a reasonable profit on the investment—or rather on the capitalization; that is to say, it is considered doubtful whether an increased production, such as to employ more workmen and supply the goods needed by the community, would result in an increased net aggregate income for the vested interests which control these industries. A reasonable profit always means, in effect, the largest obtainable profit.

All this is simple and obvious, and it should scarcely need explicit statement. It is for these business men to manage the country's industry, of course, and therefore to regulate the rate and volume of output; and also of course any regulation of the output by them will be made with a view to the needs of business; that is to say, with a view to the largest obtainable net profit, not with a view to the physical needs of these peoples who have come through the war and have made the world safe for the business of the vested interests. Should the business men in charge, by any chance aberration, stray from this straight and narrow path of business integrity, and allow the community's needs unduly to influence their management of the community's industry, they would presently find themselves discredited and would probably face insolvency. Their only salvation is a conscientious withdrawal of efficiency. All this lies in the nature of the case. It is the working of the price system, whose creatures and agents these business men are. Their case is rather pathetic, as indeed they admit quite volubly. They are not in a position to manage with a free hand, the reason being that they have in the past, under the routine requirements of the price system as it takes effect in corporation finance, taken on so large an overhead burden of fixed charges that any appreciable decrease in the net earnings of the business will bring any well-managed concern of this class face to face with bankruptcy.

At the present conjuncture, brought on by the war and its termination, the case stands somewhat in this typical shape. In the recent past earnings have been large; these large earnings (free income) have been capitalized; their capitalized value has been added to the corporate capital and covered with securities bearing a fixed income-charge; this income-charge, representing free income, has thereby become a liability on the earnings of the corporation; this liability cannot be met in case the concern's net aggregate earnings fall off in any degree; therefore prices must be kept up to such a figure as will bring the largest net aggregate return, and the only means of keeping up prices is a conscientious withdrawal of efficiency in these staple industries on which the community depends for a supply of the necessaries of life.

The business community has hopes of tiding things over by this means, but it is still a point in doubt whether the present unexampled large use of sabotage in the businesslike management of the staple industries will now suffice to bring the business community through this grave crisis without a disastrous shrinkage of its capitalization, and a consequent liquidation; but the point is not in doubt that the physical salvation of these peoples who have come through the war must in any case wait on the pecuniary salvation of these owners of corporate securities which represent free income. It is a sufficiently difficult passage. It appears that production must be curtailed in the staple industries, on pain of unprofitable prices. The case is not so desperate in those industries which have immediately to do with the production of superfluities; but even these, which depend chiefly on the custom of those kept classes to whom the free income goes, are not feeling altogether secure. For the good of business it is necessary to curtail production of the means of life, on pain of unprofitable prices, at the same time that the increasing need of all sorts of the necessaries of life must be met in some passable fashion, on pain of such popular disturbances as will always come of popular distress when it passes the limit of tolerance.

Those wise business men who are charged with administering the salutary modicum of sabotage at this grave juncture may conceivably be faced with a dubious choice between a distasteful curtailment of the free income that goes to the vested interests, on the one hand, and an unmanageable onset of popular discontent on the other hand. And in either alternative lies disaster. Present indications would seem to say that their choice will fall out according to ancient habit, that they will be likely to hold fast by an undiminished free income for the vested interests at the possible cost of any popular discontent that may be in prospect—and then, with the help of the courts and the military arm, presently make reasonable terms with any popular discontent that may arise. In which event it should all occasion no surprise or resentment, inasmuch as it would be nothing unusual or irregular and would presumably be the most expeditious way of reaching a *modus vivendi*. During the past few weeks, too, quite an unusually large number of machine guns have been sold to industrial business concerns of the larger sort, here and there, at least so they say. Business enterprise being the palladium of the Republic, it is right to take any necessary measures for its safeguarding. Price is of the essence of the case, whereas livelihood is not.

The grave emergency that has arisen out of the war and its provisional conclusion is, after all, nothing exceptional except in magnitude and severity. In substance it is the same sort of thing that goes on continually but unobtrusively and as a matter of course in ordinary times of business as usual. It is only that the extremity of the case is calling attention to itself. At the same time it serves impressively to enforce the broad proposition that a conscientious withdrawal of efficiency is the beginning of wisdom in all established business enterprise that has to do with industrial production. But it has been found that this grave interest which the vested interests always have in a salutary retardation of industry at one point or another cannot well be left altogether to the haphazard and ill-coordinated efforts of individual business concerns, each taking care of its own particular line of sabotage within its own premises. The needed sabotage can best be administered on a comprehensive plan and by a central authority, since the country's industry is of the nature of a comprehensive interlocking system, whereas the business concerns which are called on to control the motions of this industrial system will necessarily work piecemeal, in severalty and at cross-purposes. In effect, their working at cross-purposes results in a sufficiently large aggregate retardation of industry, of course, but the resulting retardation is necessarily somewhat blindly apportioned and does not converge to a neat and perspicuous outcome. Even a reasonable amount of collusion among the interested business concerns will not by itself suffice to carry on that comprehensive moving equilibrium of sabotage that is required to preserve the business community from recurrent collapse or stagnation, or to bring the nation's traffic into line with the general needs of the vested interests.

Where the national government is charged with the general care of the country's business interests, as is invariably the case among the civilized nations, it follows from the nature of the case that the nation's lawgivers and administration will have some share in administering that necessary modicum of sabotage that must always go into the day's work of carrying on industry by business methods and for business purposes. The government is in a position to penalize excessive or unwholesome traffic. So, it is always considered necessary, or at least expedient, by all sound mercantilists, as by a tariff or by subsidies, to impose and maintain a certain balance or proportion among the several branches of industry and trade that go to make up the nation's industrial system. The purpose commonly urged for measures of this class is the fuller utilization of the nation's industrial resources in material, equipment, and man power; the invariable effect is a lowered efficiency and a wasteful use of these resources, together with an increase of international jealousy. But measures of that kind are thought to be expedient by the mercantilists for these purposes—that is to say, by the statesmen of these civilized nations, for the purposes of the vested interests. The chief and nearly the sole means of maintaining such a fabricated balance and proportion among the nation's industries is to obstruct the traffic at some critical point by prohibiting or penalizing any exuberant undesirables among these branches of industry. Disallowance, in whole or in part, is the usual and standard method.

The great standing illustration of sabotage administered by the government is the protective tariff, of course. It protects certain special interests by obstructing competition from beyond the frontier. This is the main use of a national boundary. The effect of the tariff is to keep the supply of goods down and thereby keep the price up, and so to bring reasonably satisfactory dividends to those special interests which deal in the protected articles of trade, at the cost of the underlying community. A protective tariff is a typical conspiracy in restraint of trade. It brings a relatively small, though absolutely large, run of free income to the special interests which benefit by it, at a relatively, and absolutely, large cost to the underlying community, and so it gives rise to a body of vested rights and intangible assets belonging to these special interests.

Of a similar character, in so far that in effect they are in the nature of sabotage—conscientious withdrawal of efficiency—are all manner of excise and revenue-stamp regulations; although they are not always designed for that purpose. Such would be, for instance, the partial or complete prohibition of alcoholic beverages, the regulation of the trade in tobacco, opium, and other deleterious narcotics, drugs, poisons, and high explosives. Of the same nature, in effect if not in intention, are such regulations as the oleomargarine law; as also the unnecessarily costly and vexatious routine of inspection imposed on the production of industrial (denatured) alcohol, which has inured to the benefit of certain business concerns that are interested in other fuels for use in internal-combustion engines; so also the singularly vexatious and elaborately imbecile specifications that limit and discourage the use of the parcel post, for the benefit of the express companies and other carriers which have a vested interest in traffic of that kind.

It is worth noting in the same connection, although it comes in from the other side of the case, that ever since the express companies have been taken over by the federal administration there has visibly gone into effect a comprehensive system of vexation and delay in the detail conduct of their traffic, so contrived as to discredit federal control of this traffic and thereby provoke a popular sentiment in favor of its early return to private control. Much the same state of things has been in evidence in the railway traffic under similar conditions. Sabotage is serviceable as a deterrent, whether in furtherance of the administration's work or in contravention of it.

In what has just been said there is, of course, no intention to find fault with any of these uses of sabotage. It is not a question of morals and good intentions. It is always to be presumed as a matter of course that the guiding spirit in all such governmental moves to regularize the nation's affairs, whether by restraint or by incitement, is a wise solicitude for the nation's enduring gain and security. All that can be said here is that many of these wise measures of restraint and incitement are in the nature of sabotage, and that in effect they habitually, though not invariably, inure to the benefit of certain vested interests—ordinarily vested interests which bulk large in the ownership and control of the nation's resources. That these measures are quite legitimate and presumably salutary, therefore, goes without saying. In effect they are measures for hindering traffic and industry at one point or another, which may often be a wise business precaution.

During the period of the war administrative measures in the nature of sabotage have been greatly extended in scope and kind. Peculiar and imperative exigencies have had to be met, and the staple means of meeting many of these new and exceptional exigencies has quite reasonably been something in the way of avoidance, disallowance, penalization, hindrance, a conscientious withdrawal of efficiency from work that does not fall in with the purposes of the Administration. Very much as is true in private business when a situation of doubt and hazard presents itself, so also in the business of government at the present juncture of exacting demands and inconvenient limitations, the Administration has been driven to expedients of disallowance and obstruction with regard to some of the ordinary processes of life, as, for instance, in the non-essential industries. It has also appeared that the ordinary equipment and agencies for gathering and distributing news and other information have in the past developed a capacity far in excess of what can safely be permitted in time of war or of returning peace. The like is true for the ordinary facilities for public discussion of all sorts of public questions. The ordinary facilities, which may have seemed scant enough in time of peace and slack interest, had after all developed a capacity far beyond what the governmental traffic will bear in these uneasy times of war and negotiations, when men are very much on the alert to know what is going on. By a moderate use of the later improvements in the technology of transport and communication, the ordinary means of disseminating information and opinions have grown so efficient that the traffic can no longer be allowed to run at full capacity during a period of stress in the business of government. Even the mail service has proved insufferably efficient, and a selective withdrawal of efficiency has gone into effect. To speak after the analogy of private business, it has been found best to disallow such use of the mail facilities as does not inure to the benefit of the Administration in the way of good will and vested rights of usufruct.

These peremptory measures of disallowance have attracted a wide and dubious attention; but they have doubtless been of a salutary nature and intention, in some way which is not to be understood by outsiders—that is to say, by citizens of the Republic. An unguarded dissemination of information and opinions or an unduly frank canvassing of the relevant facts by these outsiders, will be a handicap on the Administration's work, and may even defeat the Administration's aims. At least so they say.

Something of much the same color has been observed elsewhere and in other times, so that all this nervously alert resort to sabotage on undesirable information and opinions is nothing novel, nor is it peculiarly democratic. The elder statesmen of the great monarchies, east and west, have long seen and approved the like. But these elder statesmen of the dynastic régime have gone to their work of sabotage on information because of a palpable division of sentiment between their government and the underlying population, such as does not exist in the advanced democratic commonwealths. The case of Imperial Germany during the period of the war is believed to show such a division of sentiment between the government and the underlying population, and also to show how such a divided sentiment on the part of a distrustful and distrusted population had best be dealt with. The method approved by German dynastic experience is sabotage, of a somewhat free-swung character, censorship, embargo on communication, and also, it is confidently alleged, elaborate misinformation.

Such procedure on the part of the dynastic statesmen of the Empire is comprehensible even to a layman. But how it all stands with those advanced democratic nations, like America, where the government is the dispassionately faithful agent and spokesman of the body of citizens, and where there can consequently be no division of aims and sentiment between the body of officials and any underlying population—all that is a more obscure and hazardous subject of speculation. Yet there has been censorship, somewhat rigorous, and there has been selective refusal of mail facilities, somewhat arbitrary, in these democratic commonwealths also, and not least in America, freely acknowledged to be the most naïvely democratic of them all. And all the while one would like to believe that it all has somehow served some useful end. It is all sufficiently perplexing.

II

The Industrial System and the Captains of Industry

It has been usual, and indeed it still is not unusual, to speak of three coordinate "factors of production": land, labor, and capital. The reason for this threefold scheme of factors in production is that there have been three recognized classes of income: rent, wages, and profits; and it has been assumed that whatever yields an income is a productive factor. This scheme has come down from the eighteenth century. It is presumed to have been true, in a general way, under the conditions which prevailed in the eighteenth century, and it has therefore also been assumed that it should continue to be natural, or normal, true in some eminent sense, under any other conditions that have come on since that time.

Seen in the light of later events this threefold plan of coordinate factors in production is notable for what it omits. It assigns no productive effect to the industrial arts, for example, for the conclusive reason that the state of the industrial arts yields no stated or ratable income to any one class of persons; it affords no legal claim to a share in the community's yearly production of goods. The state of the industrial art is a joint stock of knowledge derived from past experience, and is held and passed on as an indivisible possession of the community at large. It is the indispensable foundation of all productive industry, of course, but except for certain minute fragments covered by patent rights or trade secrets, this joint stock is no man's individual property. For this reason it has not been counted in as a factor in production. The unexampled advance of technology during the past one hundred and fifty years has now begun to call attention to its omission from the threefold plan of productive factors handed down from that earlier time.

Another omission from the scheme of factors, as it was originally drawn, was the business man. But in the course of the nineteenth century the business man came more and more obtrusively to the front and came in for a more and more generous portion of the country's yearly income—which was taken to argue that he also contributed increasingly to the yearly production of goods. So a fourth factor of production has provisionally been added to the threefold scheme, in the person of the "entrepreneur," whose wages of management are considered to measure his creative share in the production of goods, although there still is some question as to the precise part of the entrepreneur in productive industry.

"Entrepreneur" is a technical term to designate the man who takes care of the financial end of things. It covers the same fact as the more familiar "business man," but with a vague suggestion of big business rather than small. The typical entrepreneur is the corporation financier. And since the corporation financier has habitually come in for a very substantial share of the community's yearly income he has also been conceived to render a very substantial service to the community as a creative force in that productive industry out of which the yearly income arises. Indeed, it is nearly true that in current usage "producer" has come to mean "financial manager," both in the standard economic theory and in everyday speech.

There need of course be no quarrel with all this. It is a matter of usage. During the era of the machine industry—which is also the era of the commercial democracy—business men have controlled production and have managed the industry of the commonwealth for their own ends, so that the material fortunes of all the civilized peoples have continued to turn on the financial management of their business men. And during the same period not only have the conditions of life among these civilized peoples continued to be fairly tolerable on the whole, but it is also true that the industrial system which these business men have been managing for their own private gain all this time has continually been growing more efficient on the whole. Its productive capacity per unit of equipment and man power has continually grown larger. For this very creditable outcome due credit should be, as indeed it has been, given to the business community which has had the oversight of things. The efficient enlargement of industrial capacity has, of course, been due to a continued advance in technology, to a continued increase of the available natural resources, and to a continued increase of population. But the business community have also had a part in bringing all this to pass; they have always been in a position to hinder this growth, and it is only by their consent and advice that things have been enabled to go forward so far as they have gone.

This sustained advance in productive capacity, due to the continued advance in technology and in population, has also had another notable consequence. According to the Liberal principles of the eighteenth century any legally defensible receipt of income is a sure sign of productive work done. Seen in the light of this assumption, the visibly increasing productive capacity of the industrial system has enabled all men of a liberal and commercial mind not only to credit the businesslike captains of industry with having created this productive capacity, but also to overlook all that the same captains of industry have been doing in the ordinary course of business to hold productive industry in check. And it happens that all this time things have been moving in such a direction and have now gone so far that it is today quite an open question whether the businesslike management of the captains is not more occupied with checking industry than with increasing its productive capacity.

• • •

This captain of industry, typified by the corporation financier, and latterly by the investment banker, is one of the institutions that go to make up the new order of things, which has been coming on among all the civilized peoples ever since the Industrial Revolution set in. As such, as an institutional growth, his life history hitherto should be worth looking into for any one who proposes to understand the recent growth and present drift of this new economic order. The beginnings of the captain of industry are to be seen at their best among those enterprising Englishmen who made it their work to carry the industrial promise of the Revolution out into tangible performance, during the closing decades of the eighteenth and the early decades of the nineteenth century. These captains of the early time are likely to be rated as inventors, at least in a loose sense of the word. But it is more to the point that they were designers and builders of factory, mill, and mine equipment, of engines, processes, machines, and machine tools, as well as shop managers, at the same time that they took care, more or less effectually, of the financial end. Nowhere do these beginnings of the captain of industry stand out so convincingly as among the English tool-builders of that early time, who designed, tried out, built, and marketed that series of indispensable machine tools that has made the practical foundation of the mechanical industry. Something to much the same effect is due to be said for the pioneering work of the Americans along the same general lines of mechanical design and performance at a slightly later period. To men of this class the new industrial order owes much of its early success as well as of its later growth.

These men were captains of industry, entrepreneurs, in some such simple and comprehensive sense of the word as that which the economists appear to have had in mind for a hundred years after, when they have spoken of the wages of management that are due the entrepreneur for productive work done. They were a cross between a business man and an industrial expert, and the industrial expert appears to have been the more valuable half in their composition. But factory, mine, and ship owners, as well as merchants and bankers, also made up a vital part of that business community out of whose later growth and specialization the corporation financier of the nineteenth and twentieth centuries has arisen. His origins are both technological and commercial, and in that early phase of his life history which has been taken over into the traditions of economic theory and of common sense he carried on both of these lines of interest and of work in combination. That was before the large scale, the wide sweep, and the profound specialization of the advanced mechanical industry had gathered headway.

But progressively the cares of business management grew larger and more exacting, as the scale of things in business grew larger, and so the directive head of any such business concern came progressively to give his attention more and more exclusively to the "financial end." At the same time and driven by the same considerations the businesslike management of industry has progressively been shifting to the footing of corporation finance. This has brought on a further division, dividing the ownership of the industrial equipment and resources from their management. But also at the same time the industrial system, on its technological side, has been progressively growing greater and going farther in scope diversity, specialization, and complexity, as well as in productive capacity per unit of equipment and man power.

The last named item of change, the progressive increase of productive capacity, is peculiarly significant in this connection. Through the earlier and pioneering decades of the machine era it appears to have been passably true that the ordinary routine of management in industrial business was taken up with reaching out for new ways and means and speeding up production to maximum capacity. That was before standardization of processes and of unit products and fabrication of parts had been carried far, and therefore before quantity production had taken on anything like its later range and reach. And, partly because of that fact—because quantity production was then still a slight matter and greatly circumscribed, as contrasted with its later growth—the ordinary volume of output in the mechanical industries was still relatively slight and manageable. Therefore those concerns that were engaged in these industries still had a fairly open market for whatever they might turn out, a market capable of taking up any reasonable increase of output. Exceptions to this general rule occurred; as, e.g., in textiles. But the general rule stands out obtrusively through the early decades of the nineteenth century so far as regards English industry, and even more obviously in the case of America. Such an open market meant a fair chance for competitive production, without too much risk of overstocking. And running to the same effect, there was the continued increase of population and the continually increasing reach and volume of the means of transport, serving to maintain a free market for any prospective increase of output, at prices which offered a fair prospect of continued profit. In the degree in which this condition of things prevailed a reasonably free competitive production would be practicable.

The industrial situation so outlined began visibly to give way toward the middle of the nineteenth century in England, and at a correspondingly later period in America. The productive capacity of the mechanical industry was visibly overtaking the capacity of the market, so that free competition without afterthought was no longer a sound footing on which to manage production. Loosely, this critical or transitional period falls in and about the second quarter of the nineteenth century in England; elsewhere at a correspondingly later date. Of course the critical point, when business exigencies began to dictate a policy of combination and restriction, did not come at the same date in all or in most of the mechanical industries; but it seems possible to say that, by and large, the period of transition to a general rule of restriction in industry comes on at the time and for the reason so indicated.

There were also other factors engaged in that industrial situation, besides those spoken of above, less notable and less sharply defined, but enforcing limitations of the same character. Such were, e.g., a rapidly gaining obsolescence of industrial plant, due to improvements and extensions, as also the partial exhaustion of the labor supply by persistent overwork, under-feeding, and unsanitary conditions—but this applies to the English case rather than elsewhere.

In point of time this critical period in the affairs of industrial business coincides roughly with the coming in of corporation finance as the ordinary and typical method of controlling the industrial output. Of course the corporation, or company, has other uses besides the restrictive control of the output with a view to a profitable market, but it should be sufficiently obvious that the combination of ownership and centralization of control which the corporation brings about is also exceedingly convenient for that purpose. And when it appears that the general resort to corporate organization of the larger sort sets in about the time when business exigencies begin to dictate an imperative restriction of output, it is not easy to avoid the conclusion that this was one of the ends to be served by this reorganization of business enterprise. Business enterprise may fairly be said to have shifted from the footing of free-swung competitive production to that of a "conscientious withholding of efficiency," so soon and so far as corporation finance on a sufficiently large scale had come to be the controlling factor in industry. At the same time and in the same degree the discretionary control of industry, and of other business enterprise in great part, has passed into the hands of the corporation financier.

Corporate organization has continually gone forward to a larger scale and a more comprehensive coalition of forces, and at the same time, and more and more visibly, it has become the ordinary duty of the corporate management to adjust production to the requirements of the market by restricting the output to what the traffic will bear; that is to say, what will yield the largest net earnings. Under corporate management it rarely happens that production is pushed to the limit of capacity. It happens, and can happen, only rarely and intermittently. This has been true, increasingly, ever since the ordinary productive capacity of the mechanical industries seriously began to overtake and promised to exceed what the market would carry off at a reasonably profitable price. And ever since that critical turn in the affairs of industrial business—somewhere in the middle half of the nineteenth century—it has become increasingly imperative to use a wise moderation and stop down the output to such a rate and volume as the traffic will bear. The cares of business have required an increasingly undivided attention on the part of the business men, and in an ever increasing measure their day's work has come to center about a running adjustment of sabotage on production. And for this purpose, evidently, the corporate organization of this business, on an increasingly large scale, is very serviceable, since the requisite sabotage on productive industry can be effectually administered only on a large plan and with a firm hand.

• • •

"The leaders in business are men who have studied and thought all their lives. They have thus learned to decide big problems at once, basing their decisions upon their knowledge of fundamental principles."—Jeremiah W. Jenks. That is to say, the surveillance of this financial end of industrial business, and the control of the requisite running balance of sabotage, have been reduced to a routine governed by settled principles of procedure and administered by suitably trained experts in corporation finance. But under the limitations to which all human capacity is subject it follows from this increasingly exacting discipline of business administration that the business men are increasingly out of touch with that manner of thinking and those elements of knowledge that go to make up the logic and the relevant facts of the mechanical technology. Addiction to a strict and unremitting valuation of all things in terms of price and profit leaves them, by settled habit, unfit to appreciate those technological facts and values that can be formulated only in terms of tangible mechanical performance; increasingly so with every further move into a stricter addiction to businesslike management and with every further advance of the industrial system into a still wider scope and a still more diversified and more delicately balanced give and take among its interlocking members.

They are experts in prices and profits and financial manœuvres; and yet the final discretion in all questions of industrial policy continues to rest in their hands. They are by training and interest captains of finance; and yet, with no competent grasp of the industrial arts, they continue to exercise a plenary discretion as captains of industry. They are unremittingly engaged in a routine of acquisition, in which they habitually reach their ends by a shrewd restriction of output; and yet they continue to be entrusted with the community's industrial welfare, which calls for maximum production.

Such has been the situation in all the civilized countries since corporation finance has ruled industry, and until a recent date. Quite recently this settled scheme of business management has shown signs of giving way, and a new move in the organization of business enterprise has come in sight, whereby the discretionary control of industrial production is shifting still farther over to the side of finance and still farther out of touch with the requirements of maximum production. The new move is of a twofold character: (a) the financial captains of industry have been proving their industrial incompetence in a progressively convincing fashion, and (b) their own proper work of financial management has progressively taken on a character of standardized routine such as no longer calls for or admits any large measure of discretion or initiative. They have been losing touch with the management of industrial processes, at the same time that the management of corporate business has, in effect, been shifting into the hands of a bureaucratic clerical staff. The corporation financier of popular tradition is taking on the character of a chief of bureau.

The changes which have brought the corporation financier to this somewhat inglorious position of a routine administrator set in along with the early growth of corporation finance, somewhere around the middle of the nineteenth century, and they have come to a head somewhere about the passage to the twentieth century, although it is only since the latter date that the outcome is becoming at all clearly defined. When corporate organization and the consequent control of output came into bearing there were two lines of policy open to the management: (a) to maintain profitable prices by limiting the output, and (b) to maintain profits by lowering the production cost of an increased output. To some extent both of these lines were followed, but on the whole the former proved the more attractive; it involved less risk, and it required less acquaintance with the working processes of industry. At least it appears that in effect the preference was increasingly given to the former method during this half-century of financial management. For this there were good reasons. The processes of production were continually growing more extensive, diversified, complicated, and more difficult for any layman in technology to comprehend—and the corporation financier was such a layman, necessarily and increasingly so, for reasons indicated above. At the same time, owing to a continued increase of population and a continued extension of the industrial system, the net product of industry and its net earnings continued to increase independently of any creative effort on the part of the financial management. So the corporation financier, as a class, came in for an "unearned increment" of income, on the simple plan of "sitting tight." That plan is intelligible to any layman. All industrial innovation and all aggressive economy in the conduct of industry not only presumes an insight into the technological details of the industrial process, but to any other than the technological experts, who know the facts intimately, any move of that kind will appear hazardous. So the business men who have controlled industry, being laymen in all that concerns its management, have increasingly been content to let well enough alone and to get along with an ever increasing overhead charge of inefficiency, so long as they have lost nothing by it. The result has been an ever increasing volume of waste and misdirection in the use of equipment, resources, and man power throughout the industrial system.

In time, that is to say within the last few years, the resulting lag, leak, and friction in the ordinary working of this mechanical industry under business management have reached such proportions that no ordinarily intelligent outsider can help seeing them wherever he may look into the facts of the case. But it is the industrial experts, not the business men, who have finally begun to criticize this businesslike mismanagement and neglect of the ways and means of industry. And hitherto their efforts and advice have met with no cordial response from the business men in charge, who have, on the whole, continued to let well enough alone—that is to say, what is well enough for a short-sighted business policy looking to private gain, however poorly it may serve the material needs of the community. But in the meantime two things have been happening which have deranged the régime of the corporation financier: industrial experts, engineers, chemists, mineralogists, technicians of all kinds, have been drifting into more responsible positions in the industrial system and have been growing up and multiplying within the system, because the system will no longer work at all without them; and on the other hand, the large financial interests on whose support the corporation financiers have been leaning have gradually come to realize that corporation finance can best be managed as a comprehensive bureaucratic routine, and that the two pillars of the house of corporate business enterprise of the larger sort are the industrial experts and the large financial concerns that control the necessary funds; whereas the corporation financier is little more than a dubious intermediate term between these two.

• • •

One of the greater personages in American business finance took note of this situation in the late nineties and set about turning it to account for the benefit of himself and his business associates, and from that period dates a new era in American corporation finance. It was for a time spoken of loosely as the Era of Trust-Making, but that phrase does not describe it at all adequately. It should rather be called the Era of the Investment Banker, and it has come to its present stage of maturity and stability only in the course of the past quarter-century.

The characteristic features and the guiding purpose of this improved method in corporation finance are best shown by a showing of the methods and achievements of that great pioneer by whom it was inaugurated. As an illustrative case, then, the American steel business in the nineties was suffering from the continued use of out-of-date processes, equipment, and locations, from wasteful management under the control of stubbornly ignorant corporation officials, and particularly from intermittent haphazard competition and mutual sabotage between the numerous concerns which were then doing business in steel. It appears to have been the last-named difficulty that particularly claimed the attention and supplied the opportunity of the great pioneer. He can by no stretch of charity be assumed to have had even a slight acquaintance with the technological needs and shortcomings of the steel industry. But to a man of commercial vision and financial sobriety it was plain that a more comprehensive, and therefore more authoritative, organization and control of the steel business would readily obviate much of the competition which was deranging prices. The apparent purpose and the evident effect of the new and larger coalition of business interests in steel was to maintain profitable prices by a reasonable curtailment of production. A secondary and less evident effect was a more economical management of the industry, which involved some displacement of quondam corporation financiers and some introduction of industrial experts. A further, but unavowed, end to be served by the same move in each of the many enterprises in coalition undertaken by the great pioneer and by his competitors was a bonus that came to these enterprising men in the shape of an increased capitalization of the business. But the notable feature of it all as seen from the point of view of the public at large was always the stabilization of prices at a reasonably high level, such as would always assure reasonably large earnings on the increased capitalization.

Since then this manner of corporation finance has been further perfected and standardized, until it will now hold true that no large move in the field of corporation finance can be made without the advice and consent of those large funded interests that are in a position to act as investment bankers; nor does any large enterprise in corporation business ever escape from the continued control of the investment bankers in any of its larger transactions; nor can any corporate enterprise of the larger sort now continue to do business except on terms which will yield something appreciable in the way of income to the investment bankers, whose continued support is necessary to its success.

The financial interest here spoken of as the investment banker is commonly something in the way of a more or less articulate syndicate of financial houses, and it is to be added that the same financial concerns are also commonly, if not invariably, engaged or interested in commercial banking of the usual kind. So that the same well-established, half-syndicated ramification of banking houses that have been taking care of the country's commercial banking, with its center of credit and of control at the country's financial metropolis, is ready from beforehand to take over and administer the country's corporation finance on a unified plan and with a view to an equitable distribution of the country's net earnings among themselves and their clients. The more inclusive this financial organization is, of course, the more able it will be to manage the country's industrial system as an inclusive whole and prevent any hazardous innovation or experiment, as well as to limit production of the necessaries to such a volume of output as will yield the largest net return to itself and its clients.

Evidently the improved plan which has thrown the discretion and responsibility into the hands of the investment banker should make for a safe and sound conduct of business, such as will avoid fluctuations of price, and more particularly avoid any unprofitable speeding-up of productive industry. Evidently, too, the initiative has hereby passed out of the hands of the corporation financier, who has fallen into the position of a financial middleman or agent, with limited discretion and with a precariously doubtful future. But all human institutions are susceptible of improvement, and the course of improvement may now and again, as in his case, result in supersession and displacement. And doubtless it is all for the best, that is to say, for the good of business, more particularly for the profit of big business.

But now as always corporation finance is a traffic in credit; indeed, now more than ever before. Therefore to stabilize corporate business sufficiently in the hands of this inclusive quasi-syndicate of banking interests it is necessary that the credit system of the country should as a whole be administered on a unified plan and inclusively. All of which is taken care of by the same conjunction of circumstances; the same quasi-syndicate of banking interests that makes use of the country's credit in the way of corporation finance is also the guardian of the country's credit at large. From which it results that, as regards those large-scale credit extensions which are of substantial consequence, the credits and debits are, in effect, pooled within the syndicate, so that no substantial derangement of the credit situation can take effect except by the free choice of this quasi-syndicate of investment banking houses; that is to say, not except they see an advantage to themselves in allowing the credit situation to be deranged, and not beyond the point which will best serve their collective purpose as against the rest of the community. With such a closed system no extension of credit obligations or multiplication of corporate securities, with the resulting inflation of values, need bring any risk of a liquidation, since credits and debits are in effect pooled within the system. By way of parenthesis it may also be remarked that under these circumstances "credit" has no particular meaning except as a method of accounting. Credit is also one of the timeworn institutions that are due to suffer obsolescence by improvement.

This process of pooling and syndication that is remaking the world of credit and corporation finance has been greatly helped on in America by the establishment of the Federal Reserve system, while somewhat similar results have been achieved elsewhere by somewhat similar devices. That system has greatly helped to extend, facilitate, simplify, and consolidate the unified control of the country's credit arrangements, and it has very conveniently left the substantial control in the hands of those larger financial interests into whose hands the lines of control in credit and industrial business were already being gathered by force of circumstances and by sagacious management of the interested parties. By this means the substantial core of the country's credit system is gathered into a self-balanced whole, closed and unbreakable, self-insured against all risk and derangement. All of which converges to the definitive stabilization of the country's business; but since it reduces financial traffic to a riskless routine it also converges to the conceivable obsolescence of corporation finance and eventually, perhaps, of the investment banker.

III

The Captains of Finance and the Engineers

In more than one respect the industrial system of today is notably different from anything that has gone before. It is eminently a system, self-balanced and comprehensive; and it is a system of interlocking mechanical processes, rather than of skilful manipulation. It is mechanical rather than manual. It is an organization of mechanical powers and material resources, rather than of skilled craftsmen and tools; although the skilled workmen and tools are also an indispensable part of its comprehensive mechanism. It is of an impersonal nature, after the fashion of the material sciences, on which it constantly draws. It runs to "quantity production" of specialized and standardized goods and services. For all these reasons it lends itself to systematic control under the direction of industrial experts, skilled technologists, who may be called "production engineers," for want of a better term.

This industrial system runs on as an inclusive organization of many and diverse interlocking mechanical processes, interdependent and balanced among themselves in such a way that the due working of any part of it is conditioned on the due working of all the rest. Therefore it will work at its best only on condition that these industrial experts, production engineers, will work together on a common understanding; and more particularly on condition that they must not work at cross purposes. These technological specialists whose constant supervision is indispensable to the due working of the industrial system constitute the general staff of industry, whose work it is to control the strategy of production at large and to keep an oversight of the tactics of production in detail.

Such is the nature of this industrial system on whose due working depends the material welfare of all the civilized peoples. It is an inclusive system drawn on a plan of strict and comprehensive interdependence, such that, in point of material welfare, no nation and no community has anything to gain at the cost of any other nation or community. In point of material welfare, all the civilized peoples have been drawn together by the state of the industrial arts into a single going concern. And for the due working of this inclusive going concern it is essential that that corps of technological specialists who by training, insight, and interest make up the general staff of industry must have a free hand in the disposal of its available resources, in materials, equipment, and man power, regardless of any national pretensions or any vested interests. Any degree of obstruction, diversion, or withholding of any of the available industrial forces, with a view to the special gain of any nation or any investor, unavoidably brings on a dislocation of the system; which involves a disproportionate lowering of its working efficiency and therefore a disproportionate loss to the whole, and therefore a net loss to all its parts.

And all the while the statesmen are at work to divert and obstruct the working forces of this industrial system, here and there, for the special advantage of one nation and another at the cost of the rest; and the captains of finance are working, at cross purposes and in collusion, to divert whatever they can to the special gain of one vested interest and another, at any cost to the rest. So it happens that the industrial system is deliberately handicapped with dissension, misdirection, and unemployment of material resources, equipment, and man power, at every turn where the statesmen or the captains of finance can touch its mechanism; and all the civilized peoples are suffering privation together because their general staff of industrial experts are in this way required to take orders and submit to sabotage at the hands of the statesmen and the vested interests. Politics and investment are still allowed to decide matters of industrial policy which should plainly be left to the discretion of the general staff of production engineers driven by no commercial bias.

• • •

No doubt this characterization of the industrial system and its besetting tribulations will seem overdrawn. However, it is not intended to apply to any date earlier than the twentieth century, or to any backward community that still lies outside the sweep of the mechanical industry. Only gradually during the past century, while the mechanical industry has progressively been taking over the production of goods and services, and going over to quantity production, has the industrial system taken on this character of an inclusive organization of interlocking processes and interchange of materials; and it is only in the twentieth century that this cumulative progression has come to a head with such effect that this characterization is now visibly becoming true. And even now it will hold true, visibly and securely, only as applies to the leading mechanical industries, those main lines of industry that shape the main conditions of life, and in which quantity production has become the common and indispensable rule. Such are, e.g., transport and communication; the production and industrial use of coal, oil, electricity and water power; the production of steel and other metals; of wood pulp, lumber, cement and other building materials; of textiles and rubber; as also grain-milling and much of the grain-growing, together with meat-packing and a good share of the stock-raising industry.

There is, of course, a large volume of industry in many lines which has not, or only in part and doubtfully, been drawn into this network of mechanical processes and quantity production, in any direct and conclusive fashion. But these other lines of industry that still stand over on another and older plan of operation are, after all, outliers and subsidiaries of the mechanically organized industrial system, dependent on or subservient to those greater underlying industries which make up the working body of the system, and which therefore set the pace for the rest. And in the main, therefore, and as regards these greater mechanical industries on whose due working the material welfare of the community depends from day to day, this characterization will apply without material abatement.

But it should be added that even as regards these greater, primary and underlying, lines of production the system has not yet reached a fatal degree of close-knit interdependence, balance, and complication; it will still run along at a very tolerable efficiency in the face of a very appreciable amount of persistent derangement. That is to say, the industrial system at large has not yet become so delicately balanced a mechanical structure and process that the ordinary amount of derangement and sabotage necessary to the ordinary control of production by business methods will paralyze the whole outright. The industrial system is not yet sufficiently close-knit for that. And yet, that extent and degree of paralysis from which the civilized world's industry is suffering just now, due to legitimate businesslike sabotage, goes to argue that the date may not be far distant when the interlocking processes of the industrial system shall have become so closely interdependent and so delicately balanced that even the ordinary modicum of sabotage involved in the conduct of business as usual will bring the whole to a fatal collapse. The derangement and privation brought on by any well organized strike of the larger sort argues to the same effect.

In effect, the progressive advance of this industrial system towards an all-inclusive mechanical balance of interlocking processes appears to be approaching a critical pass, beyond which it will no longer be practicable to leave its control in the hands of business men working at cross purposes for private gain, or to entrust its continued administration to others than suitably trained technological experts, production engineers without a commercial interest. What these men may then do with it all is not so plain; the best they can do may not be good enough; but the negative proposition is becoming sufficiently plain, that this mechanical state of the industrial arts will not long tolerate the continued control of production by the vested interests under the current businesslike rule of incapacity by advisement.

• • •

In the beginning, that is to say during the early growth of the machine industry, and particularly in that new growth of mechanical industries which arose directly out of the Industrial Revolution, there was no marked division between the industrial experts and the business managers. That was before the new industrial system had gone far on the road of progressive specialization and complexity, and before business had reached an exactingly large scale; so that even the business men of that time, who were without special training in technological matters, would still be able to exercise something of an intelligent oversight of the whole, and to understand something of what was required in the mechanical conduct of the work which they financed and from which they drew their income. Not unusually the designers of industrial processes and equipment would then still take care of the financial end, at the same time that they managed the shop. But from an early point in the development there set in a progressive differentiation, such as to divide those who designed and administered the industrial processes from those others who designed and managed the commercial transactions and took care of the financial end. So there also set in a corresponding division of powers between the business management and the technological experts. It became the work of the technologist to determine, on technological grounds, what could be done in the way of productive industry, and to contrive ways and means of doing it; but the business management always continued to decide, on commercial grounds, how much work should be done and what kind and quality of goods and services should be produced; and the decision of the business management has always continued to be final, and has always set the limit beyond which production must not go.

With the continued growth of specialization the experts have necessarily had more and more to say in the affairs of industry; but always their findings as to what work is to be done and what ways and means are to be employed in production have had to wait on the findings of the business managers as to what will be expedient for the purpose of commercial gain. This division between business management and industrial management has continued to go forward, at a continually accelerated rate, because the special training and experience required for any passably efficient organization and direction of these industrial processes has continually grown more exacting, calling for special knowledge and abilities on the part of those who have this work to do and requiring their undivided interest and their undivided attention to the work in hand. But these specialists in technological knowledge, abilities, interest, and experience, who have increasingly come into the case in this way—inventors, designers, chemists, mineralogists, soil experts, crop specialists, production managers and engineers of many kinds and denominations—have continued to be employees of the captains of industry, that is to say, of the captains of finance, whose work it has been to commercialize the knowledge and abilities of the industrial experts and turn them to account for their own gain.

It is perhaps unnecessary to add the axiomatic corollary that the captains have always turned the technologists and their knowledge to account in this way only so far as would serve their own commercial profit, not to the extent of their ability; or to the limit set by the material circumstances; or by the needs of the community. The result has been, uniformly and as a matter of course, that the production of goods and services has advisedly been stopped short of productive capacity, by curtailment of output and by derangement of the productive system. There are two main reasons for this, and both have operated together throughout the machine era to stop industrial production increasingly short of productive capacity. (a) The commercial need of maintaining a profitable price has led to an increasingly imperative curtailment of the output, as fast as the advance of the industrial arts has enhanced the productive capacity. And (b) the continued advance of the mechanical technology has called for an ever-increasing volume and diversity of special knowledge, and so has left the businesslike captains of finance continually farther in arrears, so that they have been less and less capable of comprehending what is required in the ordinary way of industrial equipment and personnel. They have therefore, in effect, maintained prices at a profitable level by curtailment of output rather than by lowering production-cost per unit of output, because they have not had such a working acquaintance with the technological facts in the case as would enable them to form a passably sound judgment of suitable ways and means for lowering production-cost; and at the same time, being shrewd business men, they have been unable to rely on the hired-man's-loyalty of technologists whom they do not understand. The result has been a somewhat distrustful blindfold choice of processes and personnel and a consequent enforced incompetence in the management of industry, a curtailment of output below the needs of the community, below the productive capacity of the industrial system, and below what an intelligent control of production would have made commercially profitable.

Through the earlier decades of the machine era these limitations imposed on the work of the experts by the demands of profitable business and by the technical ignorance of the business men, appears not to have been a heavy handicap, whether as a hindrance to the continued development of technological knowledge or as an obstacle to its ordinary use in industry. That was before the mechanical industry had gone far in scope, complexity, and specialization; and it was also before the continued work of the technologists had pushed the industrial system to so high a productive capacity that it is forever in danger of turning out a larger product than is required for a profitable business. But gradually, with the passage of time and the advance of the industrial arts to a wider scope and a larger scale, and to an increasing specialization and standardization of processes, the technological knowledge that makes up the state of the industrial arts has called for a higher degree of that training that makes industrial specialists; and at the same time any passably efficient management of industry has of necessity drawn on them and their special abilities to an ever-increasing extent. At the same time and by the same shift of circumstances, the captains of finance, driven by an increasingly close application to the affairs of business, have been going farther out of touch with the ordinary realities of productive industry; and, it is to be admitted, they have also continued increasingly to distrust the technological specialists, whom they do not understand, but whom they can also not get along without. The captains have per force continued to employ the technologists, to make money for them, but they have done so only reluctantly, tardily, sparingly, and with a shrewd circumspection; only because and so far as they have been persuaded that the use of these technologists was indispensable to the making of money.

One outcome of this persistent and pervasive tardiness and circumspection on the part of the captains has been an incredibly and increasingly uneconomical use of material resources, and an incredibly wasteful organization of equipment and man power in those great industries where the technological advance has been most marked. In good part it was this discreditable pass, to which the leading industries had been brought by these one-eyed captains of industry, that brought the régime of the captains to an inglorious close, by shifting the initiative and discretion in this domain out of their hands into those of the investment bankers. By custom the investment bankers had occupied a position between or overlapping the duties of a broker in corporate securities and those of an underwriter of corporate flotations—such a position, in effect, as is still assigned them in the standard writings on corporation finance. The increasingly large scale of corporate enterprise, as well as the growth of a mutual understanding among these business concerns, also had its share in this new move. But about this time, too, the "consulting engineers" were coming notably into evidence in many of those lines of industry in which corporation finance has habitually been concerned.

So far as concerns the present argument the ordinary duties of these consulting engineers have been to advise the investment bankers as to the industrial and commercial soundness, past and prospective, of any enterprise that is to be underwritten. These duties have comprised a painstaking and impartial examination of the physical properties involved in any given case, as well as an equally impartial auditing of the accounts and appraisal of the commercial promise of such enterprises, for the guidance of the bankers or syndicate of bankers interested in the case as underwriters. On this ground working arrangements and a mutual understanding presently arose between the consulting engineers and those banking houses that habitually were concerned in the underwriting of corporate enterprises.

The effect of this move has been twofold: experience has brought out the fact that corporation finance, at its best and soundest, has now become a matter of comprehensive and standardized bureaucratic routine, necessarily comprising the mutual relations between various corporate concerns, and best to be taken care of by a clerical staff of trained accountants; and the same experience has put the financial houses in direct touch with the technological general staff of the industrial system, whose surveillance has become increasingly imperative to the conduct of any profitable enterprise in industry. But also, by the same token, it has appeared that the corporation financier of nineteenth-century tradition is no longer of the essence of the case in corporation finance of the larger and more responsible sort. He has, in effect, come to be no better than an idle wheel in the economic mechanism, serving only to take up some of the lubricant.

Since and so far as this shift out of the nineteenth century into the twentieth has been completed, the corporation financier has ceased to be a captain of industry and has become a lieutenant of finance; the captaincy having been taken over by the syndicated investment bankers and administered as a standardized routine of accountancy, having to do with the flotation of corporation securities and with their fluctuating values, and having also something to do with regulating the rate and volume of output in those industrial enterprises which so have passed under the hand of the investment bankers.

• • •

By and large, such is the situation of the industrial system today, and of that financial business that controls the industrial system. But this state of things is not so much an accomplished fact handed on out of the recent past; it is only that such is the culmination in which it all heads up in the immediate present, and that such is the visible drift of things into the calculable future. Only during the last few years has the state of affairs in industry been obviously falling into the shape so outlined, and it is even yet only in those larger and pace-making lines of industry which are altogether of the new technological order that the state of things has reached this finished shape. But in these larger and underlying divisions of the industrial system the present posture and drift of things is unmistakable. Meantime very much still stands over out of that régime of rule-of-thumb, competitive sabotage, and commercial logrolling, in which the businesslike captains of the old order are so altogether well at home, and which has been the best that the captains have known how to contrive for the management of that industrial system whose captains they have been. So that wherever the production experts are now taking over the management, out of the dead hand of the self-made captains, and wherever they have occasions to inquire into the established conditions of production, they find the ground cumbered with all sorts of incredible makeshifts of waste and inefficiency—such makeshifts as would perhaps pass muster with any moderately stupid elderly layman, but which look like blindfold guesswork to these men who know something of the advanced technology and its working-out.

• • •

Hitherto, then, the growth and conduct of this industrial system presents this singular outcome. The technology—the state of the industrial arts—which takes effect in this mechanical industry is in an eminent sense a joint stock of knowledge and experience held in common by the civilized peoples. It requires the use of trained and instructed workmen—born, bred, trained, and instructed at the cost of the people at large. So also it requires, with a continually more exacting insistence, a corps of highly trained and specially gifted experts, of divers and various kinds. These, too, are born, bred, and trained at the cost of the community at large, and they draw their requisite special knowledge from the community's joint stock of accumulated experience. These expert men, technologists, engineers, or whatever name may best suit them, make up the indispensable General Staff of the industrial system; and without their immediate and unremitting guidance and correction the industrial system will not work. It is a mechanically organized structure of technical processes designed, installed, and conducted by these production engineers. Without them and their constant attention the industrial equipment, the mechanical appliances of industry, will foot up to just so much junk. The material welfare of the community is unreservedly bound up with the due working of this industrial system, and therefore with its unreserved control by the engineers, who alone are competent to manage it. To do their work as it should be done these men of the industrial general staff must have a free hand, unhampered by commercial considerations and reservations; for the production of the goods and services needed by the community they neither need nor are they in any degree benefited by any supervision or interference from the side of the owners. Yet the absentee owners, now represented, in effect, by the syndicated investment bankers, continue to control the industrial experts and limit their discretion, arbitrarily, for their own commercial gain, regardless of the needs of the community.

Hitherto these men who so make up the general staff of the industrial system have not drawn together into anything like a self-directing working force; nor have they been vested with anything more than an occasional, haphazard, and tentative control of some disjointed sector of the industrial equipment, with no direct or decisive relation to that personnel of productive industry that may be called the officers of the line and the rank and file. It is still the unbroken privilege of the financial management and its financial agents to "hire and fire." The final disposition of all the industrial forces still remains in the hands of the business men, who still continue to dispose of these forces for other than industrial ends. And all the while it is an open secret that with a reasonably free hand the production experts would today readily increase the ordinary output of industry by several fold,—variously estimated at some 300 per cent. to 1200 per cent. of the current output. And what stands in the way of so increasing the ordinary output of goods and services is business as usual.

• • •

Right lately these technologists have begun to become uneasily "class-conscious" and to reflect that they together constitute the indispensable General Staff of the industrial system. Their class consciousness has taken the immediate form of a growing sense of waste and confusion in the management of industry by the financial agents of the absentee owners. They are beginning to take stock of that all-pervading mismanagement of industry that is inseparable from its control for commercial ends. All of which brings home a realization of their own shame and of damage to the common good. So the engineers are beginning to draw together and ask themselves, "What about it?"

This uneasy movement among the technologists set in, in an undefined and fortuitous way, in the closing years of the nineteenth century; when the consulting engineers, and then presently the "efficiency engineers," began to make scattered corrections in detail, which showed up the industrial incompetence of those elderly laymen who were doing a conservative business at the cost of industry. The consulting engineers of the standard type, both then and since then, are commercialized technologists, whose work it is to appraise the industrial value of any given enterprise with a view to its commercial exploitation. They are a cross between a technological specialist and a commercial agent, beset with the limitations of both and commonly not fully competent in either line. Their normal position is that of an employee of the investment bankers, on a stipend or a retainer, and it has ordinarily been their fortune to shift over in time from a technological footing to a frankly commercial one. The case of the efficiency engineers, or scientific-management experts, is somewhat similar. They too have set out to appraise, exhibit, and correct the commercial short-comings of the ordinary management of those industrial establishments which they investigate, to persuade the business men in charge how they may reasonably come in for larger net earnings by a more closely shorn exploitation of the industrial forces at their disposal. During the opening years of the new century a lively interest centered on the views and expositions of these two groups of industrial experts; and not least was the interest aroused by their exhibits of current facts indicating an all-pervading lag, leak, and friction in the industrial system, due to its disjointed and one-eyed management by commercial adventurers bent on private gain.

During these few years of the opening century the members of this informal guild of engineers at large have been taking an interest in this question of habitual mismanagement by ignorance and commercial sabotage, even apart from the commercial imbecility of it all. But it is the young rather than the old among them who see industry in any other light than its commercial value. Circumstances have decided that the older generation of the craft have become pretty well commercialized. Their habitual outlook has been shaped by a long and unbroken apprenticeship to the corporation financiers and the investment bankers; so that they still habitually see the industrial system as a contrivance for the roundabout process of making money. Accordingly, the established official Associations and Institutes of Engineers, which are officered and engineered by the elder engineers, old and young, also continue to show the commercial bias of their creators, in what they criticize and in what they propose. But the new generation which has been coming on during the present century are not similarly true to that tradition of commercial engineering that makes the technological man an awestruck lieutenant of the captain of finance.

By training, and perhaps also by native bent, the technologists find it easy and convincing to size up men and things in terms of tangible performance, without commercial afterthought, except so far as their apprenticeship to the captains of finance may have made commercial afterthought a second nature to them. Many of the younger generation are beginning to understand that engineering begins and ends in the domain of tangible performance, and that commercial expediency is another matter. Indeed, they are beginning to understand that commercial expediency has nothing better to contribute to the engineer's work than so much lag, leak, and friction. The four years' experience of the war has also been highly instructive on that head. So they are beginning to draw together on a common ground of understanding, as men who are concerned with the ways and means of tangible performance in the way of productive industry, according to the state of the industrial arts as they know them at their best; and there is a growing conviction among them that they together constitute the sufficient and indispensable general staff of the mechanical industries, on whose unhindered team-work depends the due working of the industrial system and therefore also the material welfare of the civilized peoples. So also, to these men who are trained in the stubborn logic of technology, nothing is quite real that cannot be stated in terms of tangible performance; and they are accordingly coming to understand that the whole fabric of credit and corporation finance is a tissue of make-believe.

Credit obligations and financial transactions rest on certain principles of legal formality which have been handed down from the eighteenth century, and which therefore antedate the mechanical industry and carry no secure conviction to men trained in the logic of that industry. Within this technological system of tangible performance corporation finance and all its works and gestures are completely idle; it all comes into the working scheme of the engineers only as a gratuitous intrusion which could be barred out without deranging the work at any point, provided only that men made up their mind to that effect—that is to say, provided the make-believe of absentee ownership were discontinued. Its only obvious effect on the work which the engineers have to take care of is waste of materials and retardation of the work. So the next question which the engineers are due to ask regarding this timeworn fabric of ownership, finance, sabotage, credit, and unearned income is likely to be: Why cumbers it the ground? And they are likely to find the scriptural answer ready to their hand.

It would be hazardous to surmise how, how soon, on what provocation, and with what effect the guild of engineers are due to realize that they constitute a guild, and that the material fortunes of the civilized peoples already lie loose in their hands. But it is already sufficiently plain that the industrial conditions and the drift of conviction among the engineers are drawing together to some such end.

* * *

Hitherto it has been usual to count on the interested negotiations continually carried on and never concluded between capital and labor, between the agents of the investors and the body of workmen, to bring about whatever readjustments are to be looked for in the control of productive industry and in the distribution and use of its product. These negotiations have necessarily been, and continue to be, in the nature of business transactions, bargaining for a price, since both parties to the negotiation continue to stand on the consecrated ground of ownership, free bargain, and self-help; such as the commercial wisdom of the eighteenth century saw, approved and certified it all, in the time before the coming of this perplexing industrial system. In the course of these endless negotiations between the owners and their workmen there has been some loose and provisional syndication of claims and forces on both sides; so that each of these two recognized parties to the industrial controversy has come to make up a loose-knit vested interest, and each speaks for its own special claims as a party in interest. Each is contending for some special gain for itself and trying to drive a profitable bargain for itself, and hitherto no disinterested spokesman for the community at large or for the industrial system as a going concern has seriously cut into this controversy between these contending vested interests. The outcome has been businesslike concession and compromise, in the nature of bargain and sale. It is true, during the war, and for the conduct of the war, there were some half-concerted measures taken by the Administration in the interest of the nation at large, as a belligerent; but it has always been tacitly agreed that these were extraordinary war measures, not to be countenanced in time of peace. In time of peace the accepted rule is still business as usual; that is to say, investors and workmen wrangling together on a footing of business as usual.

These negotiations have necessarily been inconclusive. So long as ownership of resources and industrial plant is allowed, or so long as it is allowed any degree of control or consideration in the conduct of industry, nothing more substantial can come of any readjustment than a concessive mitigation of the owners' interference with production. There is accordingly nothing subversive in these bouts of bargaining between the federated workmen and the syndicated owners. It is a game of chance and skill played between two contending vested interests for private gain, in which the industrial system as a going concern enters only as a victim of interested interference. Yet the material welfare of the community, and not least of the workmen, turns on the due working of this industrial system, without interference. Concessive mitigation of the right to interfere with production, on the part of either one of these vested interests, can evidently come to nothing more substantial than a concessive mitigation.

But owing to the peculiar technological character of this industrial system, with its specialized, standardized, mechanical, and highly technical interlocking processes of production, there has gradually come into being this corps of technological production specialists, into whose keeping the due functioning of the industrial system has now drifted by force of circumstance. They are, by force of circumstance, the keepers of the community's material welfare; although they have hitherto been acting, in effect, as keepers and providers of free income for the kept classes. They are thrown into the position of responsible directors of the industrial system, and by the same move they are in a position to become arbiters of the community's material welfare. They are becoming class-conscious, and they are no longer driven by a commercial interest, in any such degree as will make them a vested interest in that commercial sense in which the syndicated owners and the federated workmen are vested interests. They are, at the same time, numerically and by habitual outlook, no such heterogeneous and unwieldy body as the federated workmen, whose numbers and scattering interest has left all their endeavors substantially nugatory. In short, the engineers are in a position to make the next move.

By comparison with the population at large, including the financial powers and the kept classes, the technological specialists which come in question here are a very inconsiderable number; yet this small number is indispensable to the continued working of the productive industries. So slight are their numbers, and so sharply defined and homogeneous is their class, that a sufficiently compact and inclusive organization of their forces should arrange itself almost as a matter of course, so soon as any appreciable proportion of them shall be moved by any common purpose. And the common purpose is not far to seek, in the all-pervading industrial confusion, obstruction, waste, and retardation which business as usual continually throws in their face. At the same time they are the leaders of the industrial personnel, the workmen, of the officers of the line and the rank and file; and these are coming into a frame of mind to follow their leaders in any adventure that holds a promise of advancing the common good.

To these men, soberly trained in a spirit of tangible performance and endowed with something more than an even share of the sense of workmanship, and endowed also with the common heritage of partiality for the rule of Live and Let Live, the disallowance of an outworn and obstructive right of absentee ownership is not likely to seem a shocking infraction of the sacred realties. That customary right of ownership by virtue of which the vested interests continue to control the industrial system for the benefit of the kept classes, belongs to an older order of things than the mechanical industry. It has come out of a past that was made up of small things and traditional make-believe. For all the purposes of that scheme of tangible performance that goes to make up the technologist's world, it is without form and void. So that, given time for due irritation, it should by no means come as a surprise if the guild of engineers are provoked to put their heads together and, quite out of hand, disallow that large absentee ownership that goes to make the vested interests and to unmake the industrial system. And there stand behind them the massed and rough-handed legions of the industrial rank and file, ill at ease and looking for new things. The older commercialized generation among them would, of course, ask themselves: Why should we worry? What do we stand to gain? But the younger generation, not so hard-bitten by commercial experience, will be quite as likely to ask themselves: What do we stand to lose? And there is the patent fact that such a thing as a general strike of the technological specialists in industry need involve no more than a minute fraction of one per cent. of the population; yet it would swiftly bring a collapse of the old order and sweep the timeworn fabric of finance and absentee sabotage into the discard for good and all.

Such a catastrophe would doubtless be deplorable. It would look something like the end of the world to all those persons who take their stand with the kept classes, but it may come to seem no more than an incident of the day's work to the engineers and to the rough-handed legions of the rank and file. It is a situation which may well be deplored. But there is no gain in losing patience with a conjunction of circumstances. And it can do no harm to take stock of the situation and recognize that, by force of circumstance, it is now open to the Council of Technological Workers' and Soldiers' Deputies to make the next move, in their own way and in their own good time. When and what this move will be, if any, or even what it will be like, is not something on which a layman can hold a confident opinion. But so much seems clear, that the industrial dictatorship of the captain of finance is now held on sufferance of the engineers and is liable at any time to be discontinued at their discretion, as a matter of convenience.

IV

On the Danger of a Revolutionary Overturn

Bolshevism is a menace to the vested rights of property and privilege. Therefore the guardians of the Vested Interests have been thrown into a state of Red trepidation by the continued functioning of Soviet Russia and the continual outbreaks of the same Red distemper elsewhere on the continent of Europe. It is feared, with a nerve-shattering fear, that the same Red distemper of Bolshevism must presently infect the underlying population in America and bring on an overturn of the established order, so soon as the underlying population are in a position to take stock of the situation and make up their mind to a course of action. The situation is an uneasy one, and it contains the elements of much trouble; at least such appears to be the conviction of the Guardians of the established order. Something of the kind is felt to be due, on the grounds of the accomplished facts. So it is feared, with a nerve-shattering fear, that anything like uncolored information as to the facts in the case and anything like a free popular discussion of these facts must logically result in disaster. Hence all this unseemly trepidation.

The Guardians of the Vested Interests, official and quasi-official, have allowed their own knowledge of this sinister state of things to unseat their common sense. The run of the facts has jostled them out of the ruts, and they have gone in for a headlong policy of clamor and repression, to cover and suppress matters of fact and to shut off discussion and deliberation. And all the while the Guardians are also feverishly at work on a mobilization of such forces as may hopefully be counted on to "keep the situation in hand" in case the expected should happen. The one manifestly conclusive resolution to which the Guardians of the Vested Interests have come is that the underlying population is to be "kept in hand," in the face of any contingency. Their one settled principle of conduct appears to be, to stick at nothing; in all of which, doubtless, the Guardians mean well.

Now, the Guardians of the Vested Interests are presumably wise in discountenancing any open discussion or any free communication of ideas and opinions. It could lead to nothing more comfortable than popular irritation and distrust. The Vested Interests are known to have been actively concerned in the prosecution of the War, and there is no lack of evidence that their spokesmen have been heard in the subsequent counsels of the Peace. And, no doubt, the less that is known and said about the doings of the Vested Interests during the War and after, the better both for the public tranquility and for the continued growth and profit of the Vested Interests. Yet it is not to be overlooked that facts of such magnitude and of such urgent public concern as the manœuvres of the Vested Interests during the War and after can not be altogether happily covered over with a conspiracy of silence. Something like a middle course of temperate publicity should have seemed more to the point. It may be unfortunate, but it is none the less unavoidable, that something appreciable is bound to come to light; that is to say, something sinister.

It should be plain to all good citizens who have the cause of law and order at heart that in such a case a more genial policy of conciliatory promises and procrastination will be more to the purpose than any noisy recourse to the strong arm and the Star Chamber. A touch of history, and more particularly of contemporary history, would have given the Guardians a touch of sanity. Grown wise in all the ways and means of blamelessly defeating the unblest majority, the gentlemanly government of the British manage affairs of this kind much better. They have learned that bellicose gestures provoke ill will, and that desperate remedies should be held in reserve until needed. Whereas the Guardians of the Vested Interests in America are plainly putting things in train for a capital operation, for which there is no apparent necessity. It should be evident on slight reflection that things have not reached that fateful stage where nothing short of a capital operation can be counted on to save the life of the Vested Interests in America; not yet. And indeed, things need assuredly not reach such a stage if reasonable measures are taken to avoid undue alarm and irritation. All that is needed to keep the underlying population of America in a sweet temper is a degree of patient ambiguity and delay, something after the British pattern; and all will yet be well with the vested rights of property and privilege, for some time to come.

• • •

History teaches that no effectual popular uprising can be set afoot against an outworn institutional iniquity unless the movement effectually meets the special material requirements of the situation which provokes it; nor on the other hand can an impending popular overturn be staved off without making up one's account with those material conditions which converge to bring it on. The long history of British gentlemanly compromise, collusion, conciliation, and popular defeat, is highly instructive on that head. And it should be evident to any disinterested person, on any slight survey of the pertinent facts, that the situation in America does not now offer such a combination of circumstances as would be required for any effectual overturn of the established order or any forcible dispossession of these Vested Interests that now control the material fortunes of the American people. In short, by force of circumstances, Bolshevism is not a present menace to the Vested Interests in America; provided always that the Guardians of these Vested Interests do not go out of their way to precipitate trouble by such measures as will make Bolshevism of any complexion seem the lesser evil,—which is perhaps not a safe proviso, in view of the hysterically Red state of mind of the Guardians.

No movement for the dispossession of the Vested Interests in America can hope for even a temporary success unless it is undertaken by an organization which is competent to take over the country's productive industry as a whole, and to administer it from the start on a more efficient plan than that now pursued by the Vested Interests; and there is no such organization in sight or in immediate prospect. The nearest approach to a practicable organization of industrial forces in America, just yet, is the A. F. of L.;[1] which need only be named in order to dispel the illusion that there is anything to hope or fear in the way of a radical move at its hands. The A. F. of L. is itself one of the Vested Interests, as ready as any other to do battle for its own margin of privilege and profit. At the same time it would be a wholly chimerical fancy to believe that such an organization of workmen as the A. F. of L. could take over and manage any appreciable section of the industrial system, even if their single-minded interest in special privileges for themselves did not preclude their making a move in that direction. The Federation is not organized for production but for bargaining. It is not organized on lines that would be workable for the management of any industrial system as a whole, or of any special line of production within such a system. It is, in effect, an organization for the strategic defeat of employers and rival organizations, by recourse to enforced unemployment and obstruction; not for the production of goods and services. And it is officered by tacticians, skilled in the ways and means of bargaining with politicians and intimidating employers and employees; not by men who have any special insight into or interest in the ways and means of quantity production and traffic management. They are not, and for their purpose they need not

---

[1] American Federation of Labor

be, technicians in any conclusive sense,—and the fact should not be lost sight of that any effectual overturn, of the kind hazily contemplated by the hysterical officials, will always have to be primarily a technical affair.

In effect, the Federation is officered by safe and sane politicians, and its rank and file are votaries of "the full dinner-pail." No Guardian need worry about the Federation, and there is no other organization in sight which differs materially from the Federation in those respects which would count toward a practical move in the direction of a popular overturn,—unless a doubtful exception should be claimed for the Railroad Brotherhoods. The A. F. of L. is a business organization with a vested interest of its own; for keeping up prices and keeping down the supply, quite after the usual fashion of management by the other Vested Interests; not for managing productive industry or even for increasing the output of goods produced under any management. At the best, its purpose and ordinary business is to gain a little something for its own members at a more than proportionate cost to the rest of the community; which does not afford either the spiritual or the material ground for a popular overturn.

Nor is it the A. F. of L. or the other organizations for "collective bargaining" that come in for the comfortless attentions of the officials and of the many semi-official conspiracies in restraint of sobriety. Their nerve-shattering fears center rather on those irresponsible wayfaring men of industry who make up the I. W. W., and on the helpless and hapless alien unbelievers whose contribution to the sum total is loose talk in some foreign tongue. But if there is any assertion to be made without fear of stumbling it will be, that this flotsam of industry is not organized to take over the highly technical duties involved in the administration of the industrial system. But it is these and their like that engage the best attention of the many commissions, committees, clubs, leagues, federations, syndicates, and corporations for the chasing of wild geese under the Red flag.

• • •

Wherever the mechanical industry has taken decisive effect, as in America and in the two or three industrialized regions of Europe, the community lives from hand to mouth in such a way that its livelihood depends on the effectual working of its industrial system from day to day. In such a case a serious disturbance and derangement of the balanced process of production is always easily brought on, and it always brings immediate hardship on large sections of the community. Indeed, it is this state of things—the ease with which industry can be deranged and hardship can be brought to bear on the people at large—that constitutes the chief asset of such partisan organizations as the A. F. of L. It is a state of things which makes sabotage easy and effectual and gives it breadth and scope. But sabotage is not revolution. If it were, then the A. F. of L., the I. W. W., the Chicago Packers, and the U. S. Senate would be counted among the revolutionists.

Far-reaching sabotage, that is to say derangement of the industrial system, such as to entail hardship on the community at large or on some particular section of it, is easily brought to bear in any country that is dominated by the mechanical industry. It is commonly resorted to by both parties in any controversy between the businesslike employers and the employees. It is, in fact, an everyday expedient of business, and no serious blame attaches to its ordinary use. Under given circumstances, as, e.g., under the circumstances just now created by the return of peace, such derangement of industry and hindrance of production is an unavoidable expedient of "business as usual." And derangement of the same nature is also commonly resorted to as a means of coercion in any attempted movement of overturn. It is the simple and obvious means of initiating any revolutionary disturbance in any industrial or commercialized country. But under the existing industrial conditions, if it is to achieve even a transient success, any such revolutionary movement of reconstruction must also be in a position from the outset to overcome any degree of initial derangement in industry, whether of its own making or not, and to do constructive work of that particular kind which is called for by the present disposition of industrial forces and by the present close dependence of the community's livelihood on the due systematic working of these industrial forces. To take effect and to hold its own even for the time being, any movement of overturn must from beforehand provide for a sufficiently productive conduct of the industrial system on which the community's material welfare depends, and for a competent distribution of goods and services throughout the community. Otherwise, under existing industrial conditions, nothing more can be accomplished than an ephemeral disturbance and a transient season of accentuated hardship. Even a transient failure to make good in the management of the industrial system must immediately defeat any movement of overturn in any of the advanced industrial countries. At this point the lessons of history fail, because the present industrial system and the manner of close-knit community life enforced by this industrial system have no example in history.

This state of things, which so conditions the possibility of any revolutionary overturn, is peculiar to the advanced industrial countries; and the limitations which this state of things imposes are binding within these countries in the same measure in which these peoples are dominated by the system of mechanical industry. In contrast with this state of things, the case of Soviet Russia may be cited to show the difference. As compared with America and much of western Europe, Russia is not an industrialized region, in any decisive sense; although Russia, too, leans on the mechanical industry in a greater degree than is commonly recognized. Indeed, so considerable is the dependence of the Russians on the mechanical industry that it may yet prove to be the decisive factor in the struggle which is now going on between Soviet Russia and the Allied Powers.

Now, it is doubtless this continued success of the Soviet administration in Russia that has thrown this ecstatic scare into the Guardians of the Vested Interests in America and in the civilized countries of Europe. There is nothing to be gained by denying that the Russian Soviet has achieved a measure of success; indeed, an astonishing measure of success, considering the extremely adverse circumstances under which the Soviet has been at work. The fact may be deplored, but there it is. The Soviet has plainly been successful, in the material respect, far beyond the reports which have been allowed to pass the scrutiny of the Seven Censors and the Associated Prevarication Bureaux of the Allied Powers. And this continued success of Bolshevism in Russia—or such measure of success as it has achieved—is doubtless good ground for a reasonable degree of apprehension among good citizens elsewhere; but it does not by any means argue that anything like the same measure of success could be achieved by a revolutionary movement on the same lines in America, even in the absence of intervention from outside.

Soviet Russia has made good to the extent of maintaining itself against very great odds for some two years; and it is even yet a point in doubt whether the Allied Powers will be able to put down the Soviet by use of all the forces at their disposal and with the help of all the reactionary elements in Russia and in the neighboring countries. But the Soviet owes this measure of success to the fact that the Russian people have not yet been industrialized in anything like the same degree as their western neighbors. They have in great measure been able to fall back on an earlier, simpler, less close-knit plan of productive industry; such that any detailed part of this loose-knit Russian community is able, at a pinch, to draw its own livelihood from its own soil by its own work, without that instant and unremitting dependence on materials and wrought goods drawn from foreign ports and distant regions, that is characteristic of the advanced industrial peoples. This old-fashioned plan of home production does not involve an "industrial system" in the same exacting sense as the mechanical industry. The Russian industrial system, it is true, also runs on something of a balanced plan of give and take; it leans on the mechanical industry in some considerable degree and draws on foreign trade for many of its necessary articles of use; but for the transient time being, and for an appreciable interval of time, such a home-bred industrious population, living close to the soil and supplying its ordinary needs by home-bred handicraft methods, will be able to maintain itself in a fair state of efficiency if not in comfort, even in virtual isolation from the more advanced industrial centers and from the remoter sources of raw materials. To the ignorant,—that is to say, to the wiseacres of commerce,—this ability of the Russian people to continue alive and active under the conditions of an exemplary blockade has been a source of incredulous astonishment.

It is only as a fighting power, and then only for the purposes of an aggressive war, that such a community can count for virtually nothing in a contest with the advanced industrial nations. Such a people makes an unwieldy country to conquer from the outside. Soviet Russia is self-supporting, in a loose and comfortless way, and in this sense it is a very defensible country and may yet prove extremely difficult for the Allied Powers to subdue; but in the nature of the case there need be not the slightest shadow of apprehension that Soviet Russia can successfully take the offensive against any outside people, great or small, which has the use of the advanced mechanical industry.

The statesmen of the Allied Powers, who are now carrying on a covert war against Soviet Russia, are in a position to know this state of the case; and not least those American statesmen, who have by popular sentiment been constrained reluctantly to limit and mask their cooperation with the reactionary forces in Finland, Poland, the Ukraine, Siberia, and elsewhere. They have all been at pains diligently to inquire into the state of things in Soviet Russia; although, it is true, they have also been at pains to give out surprisingly little information,—that being much of the reason for the Seven Censors. The well-published official and semi-official apprehension of a Bolshevist offensive to be carried on beyond the Soviet frontiers may quite safely be set down as an article of statesmanlike subterfuge. The statesmen know better. What is feared in fact is infection of the Bolshevist spirit beyond the Soviet frontiers, to the detriment of those Vested Interests whose guardians these statesmen are. And on this head the apprehensions of these Elder Statesmen are not altogether groundless; for the Elder Statesmen are also in a position to know, without much inquiry, that there is no single spot or corner in civilized Europe or America where the underlying population would have anything to lose by such an overturn of the established order as would cancel the vested rights of privilege and property, whose guardians they are.

But commercialized America is not the same thing as Soviet Russia. By and large, America is an advanced industrial country, bound in the web of a fairly close-knit and inclusive industrial system. The industrial situation, and therefore the conditions of success, are radically different in the two countries in those respects that would make the outcome in any effectual revolt. So that, for better or worse, the main lines that would necessarily have to be followed in working out any practicable revolutionary movement in this country are already laid down by the material conditions of its productive industry. On provocation there might come a flare of riotous disorder; but it would come to nothing, however substantial the provocation might be, so long as the movement does not fall in with those main lines of management which the state of the industrial system requires in order to insure any sustained success. These main lines of revolutionary strategy are lines of technical organization and industrial management; essentially lines of industrial engineering; such as will fit the organization to take care of the highly technical industrial system that constitutes the indispensable material foundation of any modern civilized community. They will accordingly not only be of a profoundly different order from what may do well enough in the case of such a loose-knit and backward industrial region as Russia, but they will necessarily also be of a kind which has no close parallel in the past history of revolutionary movements. Revolutions in the eighteenth century were military and political; and the Elder Statesmen who now believe themselves to be making history still believe that revolutions can be made and unmade by the same ways and means in the twentieth century. But any substantial or effectual overturn in the twentieth century will necessarily be an industrial overturn; and by the same token, any twentieth-century revolution can be combated or neutralized only by industrial ways and means. The case of America, therefore, considered as a candidate for Bolshevism, will have to be argued on its own merits, and the argument will necessarily turn on the ways and means of productive industry as conditioned by the later growth of technology.

• • •

It has been argued, and it seems not unreasonable to believe, that the established order of business enterprise, vested rights, and commercialized nationalism, is due presently to go under in a muddle of shame and confusion, because it is no longer a practicable system of industrial management under the conditions created by the later state of the industrial arts. Twentieth-century technology has outgrown the eighteenth-century system of vested rights. The experience of the past few years teaches that the usual management of industry by business methods has become highly inefficient and wasteful, and the indications are many and obvious that any businesslike control of production and distribution is bound to run more and more consistently at cross purposes with the community's livelihood, the farther the industrial arts advance and the wider the industrial system extends. So that it is perhaps not reasonably to be questioned that Vested Interests in business are riding for a fall. But the end is not yet; although it is to be admitted, regretfully perhaps, that with every further advance in technological knowledge and practice and with every further increase in the volume and complexity of the industrial system, any businesslike control is bound to grow still more incompetent, irrelevant, and impertinent.

It would be quite hazardous to guess, just yet, how far off that consummation of commercial imbecility may be. There are those who argue that the existing system of business management is plainly due to go under within two years' time; and there are others who are ready, with equal confidence, to allow it a probable duration of several times that interval; although, it is true, these latter appear, on the whole, to be persons who are less intimately acquainted with the facts in the case. Many men experienced in the larger affairs of industrial business are in doubt as to how long things will hold together. But, one with another, these men who so are looking into the doubtful future are, somewhat apprehensively, willing to admit that there is yet something of a margin to go on; so much so that, barring accident, there should seem to be no warrant for counting at all confidently on a disastrous breakdown of the business system within anything like a two-year period. And, for the reassurance of the apprehensive Guardian of the Vested Interests, it is to be added that should such a break in the situation come while things are standing in their present shape, the outcome could assuredly not be an effectual overturn of the established order; so long as no practicable plan has been provided for taking over the management from the dead hand of the Vested Interests. Should such a self-made breakdown come at the present juncture, the outcome could, in fact, scarcely be anything more serious than an interval, essentially transient though more or less protracted, of turmoil and famine among the underlying population, together with something of a setback to the industrial system as a whole. There seems no reason to apprehend any substantial disallowance of the vested rights of property to follow from such an essentially ephemeral interlude of dissension. In fact, the tenure of the Vested Interests in America should seem to be reasonably secure, just yet.

Something in the nature of riotous discontent and factional disorder is perhaps to be looked for in the near future in this country, and there may even be some rash gesture of revolt on the part of ill-advised malcontents. Circumstances would seem to favor something of the kind. It is conservatively estimated that there is already a season of privation and uncertainty in prospect for the underlying population, which could be averted only at the cost of some substantial interference with the vested rights of the country's business men,—which should seem a highly improbable alternative, in view of that spirit of filial piety with which the public officials guard the prerogatives of business as usual. So, e.g., it is now (September, 1919) confidently expected, or rather computed, that a fuel famine is due in America during the approaching winter, for reasons of sound business management; and it is likewise to be expected that for the like reason the American transportation system is also due to go into a tangle of congestion and idleness about the same time—barring providential intervention in the way of unexampled weather conditions. But a season of famine and disorderly conduct does not constitute a revolutionary overturn of the established order; and the Vested Interests are secure in their continued usufruct of the country's industry, just yet.

This hopeful posture of things may be shown convincingly enough and with no great expenditure of argument. To this end it is proposed to pursue the argument somewhat further presently; by describing in outline what are the infirmities of the régime of the Vested Interests, which the more sanguine malcontents count on to bring that régime to an inglorious finish in the immediate future; and also to set down, likewise in outline, what would have to be the character of any organization of industrial forces which could be counted on effectually to wind up the régime of the Vested Interests and take over the management of the industrial system on a deliberate plan.

V

On the Circumstances Which Make for a Change

The state of industry, in America and in the other advanced industrial countries, will impose certain exacting conditions on any movement that aims to displace the Vested Interests. These conditions lie in the nature of things; that is to say, in the nature of the existing industrial system; and until they are met in some passable fashion, this industrial system can not be taken over in any effectual or enduring manner. And it is plain that whatever is found to be true in these respects for America will also hold true in much the same degree for the other countries that are dominated by the mechanical industry and the system of absentee ownership.

It may also confidently be set down at the outset that such an impartial review of the evidence as is here aimed at will make it appear that there need be no present apprehension of the Vested Interests' being unseated by any popular uprising in America, even if the popular irritation should rise very appreciably above its present pitch, and even if certain advocates of "direct action," here and there, should be so ill-advised as to make some rash gesture of revolt. The only present danger is that a boisterous campaign of repression and inquisition on the part of the Guardians of the Vested Interests may stir up some transient flutter of seditious disturbance.

• • •

To this end, then, it will be necessary to recall, in a summary way, those main facts of the industrial system and of the present businesslike control of this system which come immediately into the case. By way of general premise it is to be noted that the established order of business rests on absentee ownership and is managed with an eye single to the largest obtainable net return in terms of price; that is to say, it is a system of businesslike management on a commercial footing. The underlying population is dependent on the working of this industrial system for its livelihood; and their material interest therefore centers in the output and distribution of consumable goods, not in an increasing volume of earnings for the absentee owners. Hence there is a division of interest between the business community, who do business for the absentee owners, and the underlying population, who work for a living; and in the nature of the case this division of interest between the absentee owners and the underlying population is growing wider and more evident from day to day; which engenders a certain division of sentiment and a degree of mutual distrust. With it all the underlying population are still in a sufficiently deferential frame of mind toward their absentee owners, and are quite conscientiously delicate about any abatement of the free income which their owners come in for, according to the rules of the game as it is played.

The business concerns which so have the management of industry on this plan of absentee ownership are capitalized on their business capacity, not on their industrial capacity; that is to say, they are capitalized on their capacity to produce earnings, not on their capacity to produce goods. Their capitalization has, in effect, been calculated and fixed on the highest ordinary rate of earnings previously obtained; and on pain of insolvency their businesslike managers are now required to meet fixed income-charges on this capitalization. Therefore, as a proposition of safe and sane business management, prices have to be maintained or advanced.

From this businesslike requirement of meeting these fixed overhead charges on the capitalization there result certain customary lines of waste and obstruction, which are unavoidable so long as industry is managed by businesslike methods and for businesslike ends. These ordinary lines of waste and obstruction are necessarily (and blamelessly) included in the businesslike conduct of production. They are many and various in detail, but they may for convenience be classed under four heads: (a) Unemployment of material resources, equipment and man-power, in whole or in part, deliberately or through ignorance; (b) Salesmanship (includes, e.g., needless multiplication of merchants and shops, wholesale and retail, newspaper advertising and bill-boards, sales-exhibits, sales-agents, fancy packages and labels, adulteration, multiplication of brands and proprietary articles); (c) Production (and sales-cost) of superfluities and spurious goods; (d) Systematic dislocation, sabotage and duplication, due in part to businesslike strategy, in part to business-like ignorance of industrial requirements (includes, e.g., such things as cross-freights, monopolization of resources, withholding of facilities and information from business rivals whom it is thought wise to hinder or defeat). There is, of course, no blame, and no sense of blame or shame attaching to all this everyday waste and confusion that goes to make up the workday total of businesslike management. All of it is a legitimate and necessary part of the established order of business enterprise, within the law and within the ethics of the trade.

Salesmanship is the most conspicuous, and perhaps the gravest, of these wasteful and industrially futile practices that are involved in the businesslike conduct of industry; it bulks large both in its immediate cost and in its meretricious consequences. It also is altogether legitimate and indispensable in any industrial business that deals with customers, in buying or selling; which comes near saying, in all business that has to do with the production or distribution of goods or services. Indeed, salesmanship is, in a way, the whole end and substance of business enterprise; and except so far as it is managed with a constant view to profitable bargains, the production of goods is not a business proposition.

It is the elimination of profitable transactions of purchase and sale that is hoped for by any current movement looking to an overturn; and it is the same elimination of profitable bargaining that is feared, with a nerve-shattering fear, by the Guardians of the established order. Salesmanship is also the most indispensable and most meritorious of those qualities that go to make a safe and sane business man.

It is doubtless within the mark to say that, at an average, one-half the price paid for goods and services by consumers is to be set down to the account of salesmanship—that is, to sales-cost and to the net gains of salesmanship. But in many notable lines of merchandise the sales-cost will ordinarily foot up to some ten or twenty times the production-cost proper, and to not less than one hundred times the necessary cost of distribution. All this is not a matter for shame or distaste. In fact, just now more than ever, there is a clamorous and visibly growing insistence on the paramount merit and importance of salesmanship as the main stay of commerce and industry, and a strenuous demand for more extensive and more thorough training in salesmanship of a larger number of young men—at the public expense—to enable a shrewdly limited output of goods to be sold at more profitable prices—at the public cost. So also there is a visibly increasing expenditure on all manner of advertising; and the spokesmen of this enterprise in conspicuous waste are "pointing with pride" to the fact that the American business community have already spent upward of $600,000,000 on bill-boards alone within the past year, not to speak of much larger sums spent on newspapers and other printed matter for the same purpose—and the common man pays the cost.

At the same time advertising and manœuvres of salesmanlike spell-binding appear to be the only resource to which the country's business men know how to turn for relief from that tangle of difficulties into which the outbreak of a businesslike peace has precipitated the commercialized world. Increased sales-cost is to remedy the evils of under-production. In this connection it may be worth while to recall, without heat or faultfinding, that all the costly publicity that goes into sales-costs is in the nature of prevarication, when it is not good broad mendacity; and quite necessarily so. And all the while the proportion of sales-costs to production-costs goes on increasing, and the cost of living grows continually greater for the underlying population, and business necessities continue to enlarge the necessary expenditure on ways and means of salesmanship.

It is reasonable to believe that this state of things, which has been coming on gradually for some time past, will in time come to be understood and appreciated by the underlying population, at least in some degree. And it is likewise reasonable to believe that so soon as the underlying population come to realize that all this wasteful traffic of salesmanship is using up their productive forces, with nothing better to show for it than an increased cost of living, they will be driven to make some move to abate the nuisance. And just so far as this state of things is now beginning to be understood, its logical outcome is a growing distrust of the business men and all their works and words. But the underlying population is still very credulous about anything that is said or done in the name of Business, and there need be no apprehension of a mutinous outbreak, just yet. But at the same time it is evident that any plan of management which could contrive to dispense with all this expenditure on salesmanship, or that could materially reduce sales-costs, would have that much of a free margin to go on, and therefore that much of an added chance of success; and so also it is evident that any other than a businesslike management could so contrive, inasmuch as sales-costs are incurred solely for purposes of business, not for purposes of industry; they are incurred for the sake of private gain, not for the sake of productive work.

But there is in fact no present promise of a breakdown of business, due to the continued increase of sales-costs; although sales-costs are bound to go on increasing so long as the country's industry continues to be managed on anything like the present plan. In fact, salesmanship is the chief factor in that ever-increasing cost of living, which is in its turn the chief ground of prosperity among the business community and the chief source of perennial hardship and discontent among the underlying population. Still it is worth noting that the eventual elimination of salesmanship and sales-cost would lighten the burden of workday production for the underlying population by some fifty per cent. There is that much of a visible inducement to disallow that system of absentee ownership on which modern business enterprise rests; and—for what it may be worth—it is to be admitted that there is therefore that much of a drift in the existing state of things toward a revolutionary overturn looking to the unseating of the Vested Interests. But at the same time the elimination of salesmanship and all its voluminous apparatus and traffic would also cut down the capitalized income of the business community by something like one-half; and that contingency is not to be contemplated, not to say with equanimity, by the Guardians; and it is after all in the hands of these Guardians that the fortunes of the community rest. Such a move is a moral impossibility, just yet.

• • •

Closely related to the wasteful practices of salesmanship as commonly understood, if it should not rather be counted in as an extension of salesmanship, is that persistent unemployment of men, equipment, and material resources, by which the output of goods and services is kept down to the "requirements of the market," with a view to maintaining prices at a "reasonably profitable level." Such unemployment, deliberate and habitual, is one of the ordinary expedients employed in the businesslike management of industry. There is always more or less of it in ordinary times. "Reasonable earnings" could not be assured without it; because "what the traffic will bear" in the way of an output of goods is by no means the same as the productive capacity of the industrial system; still less is it the same as the total consumptive needs of the community; in fact, it does not visibly tend to coincide with either. It is more particularly in times of popular distress, such as the present year, when the current output of goods is not nearly sufficient to cover the consumptive needs of the community, that considerations of business strategy call for a wise unemployment of the country's productive forces. At the same time, such businesslike unemployment of equipment and man power is the most obvious cause of popular distress.

All this is well known to the Guardians of the Vested Interests, and their knowledge of it is, quite reasonably, a source of uneasiness to them. But they see no help for it; and indeed there is no help for it within the framework of "business as usual," since it is the essence of business as usual. So also, the Guardians are aware that this businesslike sabotage on productive industry is a fruitful source of discontent and distrust among the underlying population who suffer the inconvenience of it all; and they are beset with the abiding fear that the underlying population may shortly be provoked into disallowing those Vested Interests for whose benefit this deliberate and habitual sabotage on production is carried on. It is felt that here again is a sufficient reason why the businesslike management of industry should be discontinued; which is the same as saying that here again is a visibly sufficient reason for such a revolutionary overturn as will close out the Old Order of absentee ownership and capitalized income. It is also evident that any plan which shall contrive to dispense with this deliberate and habitual unemployment of men and equipment will have that much more of a margin to go on, both in respect of practical efficiency and in respect of popular tolerance; and evidently, too, any other than a businesslike management of industry can so contrive, as a matter of course; inasmuch as any such unbusinesslike administration—as, e.g., the Soviet—will be relieved of the businesslike manager's blackest bug-bear, "a reasonably profitable level of prices."

But for all that, those shudderingly sanguine persons who

are looking for a dissolution of the system of absentee ownership within two years' time are not counting on salesmanlike waste and businesslike sabotage to bring on the collapse, so much as they count on the item listed under (d) above—the systematic dislocation and all-round defeat of productive industry which is due in part to shrewd manœuvres of businesslike strategy, in part to the habitual ignorance of business men touching the systematic requirements of the industrial system as a whole. The shrewd worldly wisdom of the businesslike managers, looking consistently to the main chance, works in harmoniously with their trained ignorance on matters of technology, to bring about what amounts to effectual team-work for the defeat of the country's industrial system as a going concern. Yet doubtless this sinister hope of a collapse within two years is too sanguine. Doubtless the underlying population can be counted on stolidly to put up with what they are so well used to, just yet; more particularly so long as they are not in the habit of thinking about these things at all. Nor does it seem reasonable to believe that this all-pervading waste and confusion of industrial forces will of itself bring the business organization to a collapse within so short a time.

It is true, the industrial system is continually growing, in volume and complication; and with every new extension of its scope and range, and with every added increment of technological practice that goes into effect, there comes a new and urgent opportunity for the business men in control to extend and speed up their strategy of mutual obstruction and defeat; it is all in the day's work. As the industrial system grows larger and more closely interwoven it offers continually larger and more enticing opportunities for such businesslike manœuvres as will effectually derange the system at the same time that they bring the desired tactical defeat on some business rival; whereby the successful business strategist is enabled to get a little something for nothing at a constantly increasing cost to the community at large. With every increment of growth and maturity the country's industrial system becomes more delicately balanced, more intricately bound in a web of industrial give and take, more sensitive to far-reaching derangement by any local dislocation, more widely and instantly responsive to any failure of the due correlation at any point; and by the same move the captains of industry, to whose care the interests of absentee ownership are entrusted, are enabled, or rather they are driven by the necessities of competitive business, to plan their strategy of mutual defeat and derangement on larger and more intricate lines, with an ever wider reach and a more massive mobilization of forces. From which follows an ever increasing insecurity of work and output from day to day and an increased assurance of general loss and disability in the long run; incidentally coupled with increased hardship for the underlying population, which comes in all along as a subsidiary matter of course, unfortunate but unavoidable. It is this visibly growing failure of the present businesslike management to come up to the industrial necessities of the case; its unfitness to take anything like reasonable care of the needed correlation of industrial forces within the system; its continual working at cross purposes in the allocation of energy resources, materials, and man power—it is this fact, that any businesslike management of necessity runs at cross purposes with the larger technical realities of the industrial system, that chiefly goes to persuade apprehensive persons that the régime of business enterprise is fast approaching the limit of tolerance. So it is held by many that this existing system of absentee ownership must presently break down and precipitate the abdication of the Vested Interests, under conviction of total imbecility.

• • •

The theory on which these apprehensive persons proceed appears to be substantially sound, so far as it goes, but they reach an unguardedly desperate conclusion because they overlook one of the main facts of the case. There is no reasonable exception to be taken to the statement that the country's industrial system is forever growing more extensive and more complex; that it is continually taking on more of the character of a close-knit, interwoven, systematic whole; a delicately balanced moving equilibrium of working parts, no one of which can do its work by itself at all, and none of which can do its share of the work well except in close correlation with all the rest. At the same time it is also true that, in the commercialized nature of things, the businesslike management of industry is forever playing fast and loose with this delicately balanced moving equilibrium of forces, on which the livelihood of the underlying population depends from day to day; more particularly is this true for that large-scale business enterprise that rests on absentee ownership and makes up the country's greater Vested Interests. But to all this it is to be added, as a corrective and a main factor in the case, that this system of mechanical industry is an extremely efficient contrivance for the production of goods and services, even when, as usual, the business men, for business reasons, will allow it to work only under a large handicap of unemployment and obstructive tactics. Hitherto the margin for error, that is to say for wasteful strategy and obstructive ignorance, has been very wide; so wide that it has saved the life of the Vested Interests; and it is accordingly by no means confidently to be believed that all these ampler opportunities for swift and wide-reaching derangement will enable the strategy of business enterprise to bring on a disastrous collapse, just yet.

It is true, if the country's productive industry were competently organized as a systematic whole, and were then managed by competent technicians with an eye single to maximum production of goods and services; instead of, as now, being manhandled by ignorant business men with an eye single to maximum profits; the resulting output of goods and services would doubtless exceed the current output by several hundred per cent. But then, none of all that is necessary to save the established order of things. All that is required is a decent modicum of efficiency, very far short of the theoretical maximum production. In effect, the community is in the habit of getting along contentedly on something appreciably less than one-half the output which its industrial equipment would turn out if it were working uninterruptedly at full capacity; even when, as usual, something like one-half of the actual output is consumed in wasteful superfluities. The margin for waste and error is very wide, fortunately; and, in effect, a more patient and more inclusive survey of the facts in the case would suffice to show that the tenure of the Vested Interests is reasonably secure just yet; at least in so far as it turns on considerations of this nature.

There is, of course, the chance, and it is by no means a remote chance, that the rapidly increasing volume and complexity of the industrial system may presently bring the country's industry into such a ticklish state of unstable equilibrium that even a reasonable modicum of willful derangement can no longer be tolerated, even for the most urgent and most legitimate reasons of businesslike strategy and vested rights. In time, such an outcome is presumably due to be looked for. There is, indeed, no lack of evidence that the advanced industrial countries are approaching such a state of things, America among the rest. The margin for error and wasteful strategy is, in effect, being continually narrowed by the further advance of the industrial arts. With every further advance in the way of specialization and standardization, in point of kind, quantity, quality, and time, the tolerance of the system as a whole under any strategic maladjustment grows continually narrower.

How soon the limit of tolerance for willful derangement is due to be reached, would be a hazardous topic of speculation. There is now a fair prospect that the coming winter may throw some light on that dark question; but this is not saying that the end is in sight. What is here insisted on is that that sinister eventuality lies yet in the future, although it may be in the calculable future. So also it is well to keep in mind that even a fairly disastrous collapse of the existing system of businesslike management need by no means prove fatal to the Vested Interests, just yet; not so long as there is no competent organization ready to take their place and administer the country's industry on a more reasonable plan. It is necessarily a question of alternatives.

In all this argument that runs on perennial dislocation and cross purposes, it is assumed that the existing businesslike management of industry is of a competitive nature and necessarily moves on lines of competitive strategy. As a subsidiary premise it is, of course, also assumed that the captains of industry who have the direction of this competitive strategy are ordinarily sufficiently ill informed on technological matters to go wrong, industrially speaking, even with the most pacific and benevolent intentions. They are laymen in all that concerns the technical demands of industrial production. This latter, and minor, assumption therefore need not be argued; it is sufficiently notorious. On the other hand, the first assumption spoken of above, that current business enterprise is of a competitive nature, is likely to be questioned by many who believe themselves to be familiar with the facts in the case. It is argued, by one and another, that the country's business concerns have entered into consolidations, coalitions, understandings and working arrangements among themselves—syndicates, trusts, pools, combinations, interlocking directorates, gentlemen's agreements, employers' unions—to such an extent as virtually to cover the field of that large-scale business that sets the pace and governs the movements of the rest; and that where combination takes effect in this way, competition ceases. So also it will be argued that where there has been no formal coalition of interests the business men in charge will still commonly act in collusion, with much the same result. The suggestion is also ready to hand that in so far as businesslike sabotage of this competitive order is still to be met with, it can all be corrected by such a further consolidation of interests as will do away with all occasion for competitive cross purposes within the industrial system.

It is not easy to see just how far that line of argument would lead; but to make it effective and to cover the case it would plainly have to result in so wide a coalition of interests and pooling of management as would, in effect, eliminate all occasion for businesslike management within the system, and leave the underlying population quite unreservedly at the disposal of the resulting coalition of interests—an outcome which is presumably not contemplated. And even so, the argument takes account of only one strand in that three-ply rope that goes to fashion the fatal noose. The remaining two are stout enough, and they have not been touched. It is true, economists and others who have canvassed this matter of competition have commonly given their attention to this one line of competition alone—between rival commercial interests—because this competition is conceived to be natural and normal and to serve the common good. But there remains (a) the competition between those business men who buy cheap and sell dear and the underlying population from and to whom they buy cheap and sell dear, and (b) the competition between the captains of industry and those absentee owners in whose name and with whose funds the captains do business. In the typical case, modern business enterprise takes the corporate form, is organized on credit, and therefore rests on absentee ownership; from which it follows that in all large-scale business the owners are not the same persons as the managers, nor does the interest of the manager commonly coincide with that of his absentee owners, particularly in the modern "big business."

So it follows that even a coalition of Vested Interests which should be virtually all-inclusive, would still have to make up its account with "what the traffic will bear," that is to say what will bring the largest net income in terms of price; that is to say, the coalition would still be under the competitive necessity of buying cheap and selling dear, to the best of its ability and with the use of all the facilities which its dominant position in the market would give. The coalition, therefore, would still be under the necessity of shrewdly limiting the output of goods and services to such a rate and volume as will maintain or advance prices; and also to vary its manipulation of prices and supply from place to place and from time to time, to turn an honest penny; which leaves the case very near the point of beginning. But then, such a remedy for these infelicities of the competitive system will probably be admitted to be chimerical, without argument.

But what is more to the point is the fact, known even when it is not avowed, that the consolidations which have been effected hitherto have not eliminated competition, nor have they changed the character of the competitive strategy employed, although they have altered its scale and methods. What can be said is that the underlying corporations of the holding companies, e.g., are no longer competitors among themselves on the ancient footing. But strategic dislocation and cross purposes continue to be the order of the day in the businesslike management of industry; and the volume of habitual unemployment, whether of equipment or of man power, continues undiminished and unashamed—which is after all a major count in the case.

It is well to recognize what the business men among themselves always recognize as a matter of course, that business is in the last analysis always carried on for the private advantage of the individual business men who carry it on. And these enterprising persons, being business men, will always be competitors for gain among themselves, however much and well they may combine for a common purpose as against the rest of the community. The end and aim of any gainful enterprise carried through in common is always the division of the joint gains, and in this division the joint participants always figure as competitors. The syndicates, coalitions, corporations, consolidations of interests, so entered into in the pursuit of gain are, in effect, in the nature of conspiracies between business men each seeking his own advantage at the cost of any whom it may concern. There is no ulterior solidarity of interests among the participants in such a joint enterprise.

By way of illustration, what is set forth in the voluminous testimony taken in the Colton case, before the California courts, having to do with the affairs of the Southern Pacific and its subsidiaries, will show in what fashion the businesslike incentives of associated individuals may be expected to work out in the partition of benefits within a given coalition. And not only is there no abiding solidarity of interests between the several participants in such a joint enterprise, so far as regards the final division of the spoils, but it is also true that the business interest of the manager in charge of such a syndicate of absentee ownership will not coincide with the collective interest of the coalition as a going concern. As an illustrative instance may be cited the testimony of the great president of the two Great Northern railways, taken before a Congressional commission, wherein it is explained somewhat fully that for something like a quarter-century the two great roads under his management had never come in for reasonable earnings on their invested capital. And it is a matter of common notoriety, although it was charitably not brought out in the hearings of the commission, that during his incumbency as manager of the two great railway systems this enterprising railway president had by thrift and management increased his own private possessions from $20 to something variously estimated at $150,000,000 to $200,000,000; while his two chief associates in this adventure had retired from the management on a similarly comfortable footing; so notably comfortable, indeed, as to have merited a couple of very decent peerages under the British crown.

In effect, there still is an open call for shrewd personal strategy at the cost of any whom it may concern; all the while that there is also a very appreciable measure of collusion among the Vested Interests, at the cost of any whom it may concern. Business is still competitive business, competitive pursuit of private gain; as how should it not be? seeing that the incentive to all business is after all private gain at the cost of any whom it may concern.

• • •

By reason of doctrinal consistency and loyalty to tradition, the certified economists have habitually described business enterprise as a rational arrangement for administering the country's industrial system and assuring a full and equitable distribution of consumable goods to the consumers. There need be no quarrel with that view. But it is only fair to enter the reservation that, considered as an arrangement for administering the country's industrial system, business enterprise based on absentee ownership has the defects of its qualities; and these defects of this good old plan are now calling attention to themselves. Hitherto, and ever since the mechanical industry first came into the dominant place in this industrial system, the defects of this businesslike management of industry have continually been encroaching more and more on its qualities. It took its rise as a system of management by the owners of the industrial equipment, and it has in its riper years grown into a system of absentee ownership managed by quasi-responsible financial agents. Having begun as an industrial community which centered about an open market, it has matured into a community of Vested Interests whose vested right it is to keep up prices by a short supply in a closed market. There is no extravagance in saying that, by and large, this arrangement for controlling the production and distribution of goods and services through the agency of absentee ownership has now come to be, in the main, a blundering muddle of defects. For the purpose in hand, that is to say with a view to the probable chance of any revolutionary overturn, this may serve as a fair characterization of the régime of the Vested Interests; whose continued rule is now believed by their Guardians to be threatened by a popular uprising in the nature of Bolshevism.

Now, as to the country's industrial system which is manhandled on this businesslike plan; it is a comprehensive and balanced scheme of technological administration. Industry of this modern sort—mechanical, specialized, standardized, running to quantity production, drawn on a large scale—is highly productive; provided always that the necessary conditions of its working are met in some passable fashion. These necessary conditions of productive industry are of a well-defined technical character, and they are growing more and more exacting with every farther advance in the industrial arts. This mechanical industry draws always more and more largely and urgently on the natural sources of mechanical power, and it necessarily makes use of an ever increasingly wide and varied range of materials, drawn from all latitudes and all geographical regions, in spite of obstructive national frontiers and patriotic animosities; for the mechanical technology is impersonal and dispassionate, and its end is very simply to serve human needs, without fear or favor or respect of persons, prerogatives, or politics. It makes up an industrial system of an unexampled character—a mechanically balanced and interlocking system of work to be done, the prime requisite of whose working is a painstaking and intelligent co-ordination of the processes at work, and an equally painstaking allocation of mechanical power and materials. The foundation and driving force of it all is a massive body by technological knowledge, of a highly impersonal and altogether unbusinesslike nature, running in close contact with the material sciences, on which it draws freely at every turn—exactingly specialized, endlessly detailed, reaching out into all domains of empirical fact.

Such is the system of productive work which has grown out of the Industrial Revolution, and on the full and free run of which the material welfare of all the civilized peoples now depends from day to day. Any defect or hindrance in its technical administration, any intrusion of nontechnical considerations, any failure or obstruction at any point, unavoidably results in a disproportionate set-back to the balanced whole and brings a disproportionate burden of privation on all these peoples whose productive industry has come within the sweep of the system.

It follows that those gifted, trained, and experienced technicians who now are in possession of the requisite technological information and experience are the first and instantly indispensable factor in the everyday work of carrying on the country's productive industry. They now constitute the General Staff of the industrial system, in fact; whatever law and custom may formally say in protest. The "captains of industry" may still vaingloriously claim that distinction, and law and custom still countenance their claim; but the captains have no technological value, in fact.

Therefore any question of a revolutionary overturn, in America or in any other of the advanced industrial countries, resolves itself in practical fact into a question of what the guild of technicians will do. In effect it is a question whether the discretion and responsibility in the management of the country's industry shall pass from the financiers, who speak for the Vested Interests, to the technicians, who speak for the industrial system as a going concern. There is no third party qualified to make a colorable bid, or able to make good its pretensions if it should make a bid. So long as the vested rights of absentee ownership remain intact, the financial powers—that is to say the Vested Interests—will continue to dispose of the country's industrial forces for their own profit; and so soon, or so far, as these vested rights give way, the control of the people's material welfare will pass into the hands of the technicians. There is no third party.

The chances of anything like a Soviet in America, therefore, are the chances of a Soviet of technicians. And, to the due comfort of the Guardians of the Vested Interests and the good citizens who make up their background, it can be shown that anything like a Soviet of Technicians is at the most a remote contingency in America.

It is true, so long as no such change of base is made, what is confidently to be looked for is a régime of continued and increasing shame and confusion, hardship and dissension, unemployment and privation, waste and insecurity of person and property—such as the rule of the Vested Interests in business has already made increasingly familiar to all the civilized peoples. But the vested rights of absentee ownership are still embedded in the sentiments of the underlying population, and still continue to be the Palladium of the Republic; and the assertion is still quite safe that anything like a Soviet of Technicians is not a present menace to the Vested Interests in America.

By settled habit the technicians, the engineers and industrial experts, are a harmless and docile sort, well fed on the whole, and somewhat placidly content with the "full dinner-pail" which the lieutenants of the Vested Interests habitually allow them. It is true, they constitute the indispensable General Staff of that industrial system which feeds the Vested Interests; but hitherto at least, they have had nothing to say in the planning and direction of this industrial system, except as employees in the pay of the financiers. They have, hitherto, been quite unreflectingly content to work piecemeal, without much of an understanding among themselves, unreservedly doing job-work for the Vested Interests; and they have without much reflection lent themselves and their technical powers freely to the obstructive tactics of the captains of industry; all the while that the training which makes them technicians is but a specialized extension of that joint stock of technological knowledge that has been carried forward out of the past by the community at large.

But it remains true that they and their dear-bought knowledge of ways and means—dear-bought on the part of the underlying community—are the pillars of that house of industry in which the Vested Interests continue to live. Without their continued and unremitting supervision and direction the industrial system would cease to be a working system at all; whereas it is not easy to see how the elimination of the existing businesslike control could bring anything but relief and heightened efficiency to this working system. The technicians are indispensable to productive industry of this mechanical sort; the Vested Interests and their absentee owners are not. The technicians are indispensable to the Vested Interests and their absentee owners, as a working force without which there would be no industrial output to control or divide; whereas the Vested Interests and their absentee owners are of no material consequence to the technicians and their work, except as an extraneous interference and obstruction.

It follows that the material welfare of all the advanced industrial peoples rests in the hands of these technicians, if they will only see it that way, take counsel together, constitute themselves the self-directing General Staff of the country's industry, and dispense with the interference of the lieutenants of the absentee owners. Already they are strategically in a position to take the lead and impose their own terms of leadership, so soon as they, or a decisive number of them, shall reach a common understanding to that effect and agree on a plan of action.

But there is assuredly no present promise of the technicians' turning their insight and common sense to such a use. There need be no present apprehension. The technicians are a "safe and sane" lot, on the whole; and they are pretty well commercialized, particularly the older generation, who speak with authority and conviction, and to whom the younger generation of engineers defer, on the whole, with such a degree of filial piety as should go far to reassure all good citizens. And herein lies the present security of the Vested Interests, as well as the fatuity of any present alarm about Bolshevism and the like; for the whole-hearted co-operation of the technicians would be as indispensable to any effectual movement of overturn as their unwavering service in the employ of the Vested Interests is indispensable to the maintenance of the established order.

VI

A Memorandum on a Practicable Soviet of Technicians

It is the purpose of this memorandum to show, in an objective way, that under existing circumstances there need be no fear, and no hope, of an effectual revolutionary overturn in America, such as would unsettle the established order and unseat those Vested Interests that now control the country's industrial system. In an earlier paper (*The Dial*, October 4) it has been argued that no effectual move in the direction of such an overturn can be made except on the initiative and under the direction of the country's technicians, taking action in common and on a concerted plan. Notoriously, no move of this nature has been made hitherto, nor is there evidence that anything of the kind has been contemplated by the technicians. They still are consistently loyal, with something more than a hired-man's loyalty, to the established order of commercial profit and absentee ownership. And any adequate plan of concerted action, such as would be required for the enterprise in question, is not a small matter that can be arranged between two days.

Any plan of action that shall hope to meet the requirements of the case in any passable fashion must necessarily have the benefit of mature deliberation among the technicians who are competent to initiate such an enterprise; it must engage the intelligent co-operation of several thousand technically trained men scattered over the face of the country, in one industry and another; must carry out a passably complete cadastration of the country's industrial forces; must set up practicable organization tables covering the country's industry in some detail,—energy-resources, materials, and man power; and it must also engage the aggressive support of the trained men at work in transportation, mining, and the greater mechanical industries. These are initial requirements, indispensable to the initiation of any enterprise of the kind in such an industrial country as America; and so soon as this is called to mind it will be realised that any fear of an effectual move in this direction at present is quite chimerical. So that, in fact, it may be set down without a touch of ambiguity that absentee ownership is secure, just yet.

Therefore, to show conclusively and in an objective way how remote any contingency of this nature still is, it is here proposed to set out in a summary fashion the main lines which any such concerted plan of action would have to follow, and what will of necessity be the manner of organization which alone can hope to take over the industrial system, following the eventual abdication or dispossession of the Vested Interests and their absentee owners. And, by way of parenthesis, it is always the self-made though reluctant abdication of the Vested Interests and their absentee owners, rather than their forcible dispossession, that is to be looked for as a reasonably probable event in the calculable future. It should, in effect, cause no surprise to find that they will, in a sense, eliminate themselves, by letting go quite involuntarily after the industrial situation gets quite beyond their control. In fact, they have, in the present difficult juncture, already sufficiently shown their unfitness to take care of the country's material welfare,—which is after all the only ground on which they can set up a colorable claim to their vested rights. At the same time something like an opening bid for a bargain of abdication has already come in from more than one quarter. So that a discontinuance of the existing system of absentee ownership, on one plan or another, is no longer to be considered a purely speculative novelty; and an objective canvass of the manner of organization that is to be looked to to take the place of the control now exercised by the Vested Interests—in the event of their prospective abdication—should accordingly have some present interest, even apart from its bearing on the moot question of any forcible disruption of the established system of absentee ownership.

• • •

As a matter of course, the powers and duties of the incoming directorate will be of a technological nature, in the main if not altogether; inasmuch as the purpose of its coming into control is the care of the community's material welfare by a more competent management of the country's industrial system. It may be added that even in the unexpected event that the contemplated overturn should, in the beginning, meet with armed opposition from the partisans of the old order, it will still be true that the duties of the incoming directorate will be of a technological character, in the main; inasmuch as warlike operations are also now substantially a matter of technology, both in the immediate conduct of hostilities and in the still more urgent work of material support and supply.

The incoming industrial order is designed to correct the shortcomings of the old. The duties and powers of the incoming directorate will accordingly converge on those points in the administration of industry where the old order has most signally fallen short; that is to say, on the due allocation of resources and a consequent full and reasonably proportioned employment of the available equipment and man power; on the avoidance of waste and duplication of work; and on an equitable and sufficient supply of goods and services to consumers. Evidently the most immediate and most urgent work to be taken over by the incoming directorate is that for want of which under the old order the industrial system has been working slack and at cross purposes; that is to say the due allocation of available resources, in power, equipment, and materials, among the greater primary industries. For this necessary work of allocation there has been substantially no provision under the old order.

To carry on this allocation, the country's transportation system must be placed at the disposal of the same staff that has the work of allocation to do; since, under modern conditions, any such allocation will take effect only by use of the transportation system. But, by the same token, the effectual control of the distribution of goods to consumers will also necessarily fall into the same hands; since the traffic in consumable goods is also a matter of transportation, in the main.

On these considerations, which would only be reenforced by a more detailed inquiry into the work to be done, the central directorate will apparently take the shape of a loosely tripartite executive council, with power to act in matters of industrial administration; the council to include technicians whose qualifications enable them to be called Resource Engineers, together with similarly competent spokesmen of the transportation system and of the distributive traffic in finished products and services. With a view to efficiency and expedition, the executive council will presumably not be a numerous body; although its staff of intelligence and advice may be expected to be fairly large, and it will be guided by current consultation with the accredited spokesmen (deputies, commissioners, executives, or whatever they may be called) of the several main subdivisions of productive industry, transportation, and distributive traffic.

Armed with these powers and working in due consultation with a sufficient ramification of sub-centers and local councils, this industrial directorate should be in a position to avoid virtually all unemployment of serviceable equipment and man power on the one hand, and all local or seasonal scarcity on the other hand. The main line of duties indicated by the character of the work incumbent on the directorate, as well as the main line of qualifications in its personnel, both executive and advisory, is such as will call for the services of Production Engineers, to use a term which is coming into use. But it is also evident that in its continued work of planning and advisement the directorate will require the services of an appreciable number of consulting economists; men who are qualified to be called Production Economists.

The profession now includes men with the requisite qualifications, although it cannot be said that the gild of economists is made up of such men in the main. Quite blamelessly, the economists have, by tradition and by force of commercial pressure, habitually gone in for a theoretical inquiry into the ways and means of salesmanship, financial traffic, and the distribution of income and property, rather than a study of the industrial system considered as a ways and means of producing goods and services. Yet there now are, after all, especially among the younger generation, an appreciable number, perhaps an adequate number, of economists who have learned that "business" is not "industry" and that investment is not production. And, here as always, the best is good enough, perforce.

"Consulting economists" of this order are a necessary adjunct to the personnel of the central directorate, because the technical training that goes to make a resource engineer, or a production engineer, or indeed a competent industrial expert in any line of specialization, is not of a kind to give him the requisite sure and facile insight into the play of economic forces at large; and as a matter of notorious fact, very few of the technicians have gone at all far afield to acquaint themselves with anything more to the point in this connection than the half-forgotten commonplaces of the old order. The "consulting economist" is accordingly necessary to cover an otherwise uncovered joint in the new articulation of things. His place in the scheme is analogous to the part which legal counsel now plays in the manœuvres of diplomatists and statesmen; and the discretionary personnel of the incoming directorate are to be, in effect, something in the way of industrial statesmen under the new order.

There is also a certain general reservation to be made with regard to personnel, which may conveniently be spoken of at this point. To avoid persistent confusion and prospective defeat, it will be necessary to exclude from all positions of trust and executive responsibility all persons who have been trained for business or who have had experience in business undertakings of the larger sort. This will apply generally, throughout the administrative scheme, although it will apply more imperatively as regards the responsible personnel of the directorate, central and subordinate, together with their staff of intelligence and advice, wherever judgment and insight are essential. What is wanted is training in the ways and means of productive industry, not in the ways and means of salesmanship and profitable investment.

By force of habit, men trained to a businesslike view of what is right and real will be irretrievably biassed against any plan of production and distribution that is not drawn in terms of commercial profit and loss and does not provide a margin of free income to go to absentee owners. The personal exceptions to the rule are apparently very few. But this one point is after all of relatively minor consequence. What is more to the point in the same connection is that the commercial bias induced by their training in businesslike ways of thinking leaves them incapable of anything like an effectual insight into the use of resources or the needs and aims of productive industry, in any other terms than those of commercial profit and loss. Their units and standards of valuation and accountancy are units and standards of price, and of private gain in terms of price; whereas for any scheme of productive industry which runs, not on salesmanship and earnings, but on tangible performances and tangible benefit to the community at large, the valuations and accountancy of salesmanship and earnings are misleading. With the best and most benevolent intentions, men so trained will unavoidably make their appraisals of production and their disposition of productive forces in the only practical terms with which they are familiar, the terms of commercial accountancy; which is the same as saying, the accountancy of absentee ownership and free income; all of which it is the abiding purpose of the projected plan to displace. For the purposes of this projected new order of production, therefore, the experienced and capable business men are at the best to be rated as well-intentioned deaf-mute blind men. Their wisest judgment and sincerest endeavors become meaningless and misguided so soon as the controlling purpose of industry shifts from the footing of profits on absentee investment to that of a serviceable output of goods.

All this abjuration of business principles and businesslike sagacity may appear to be a taking of precautions about a vacant formality; but it is as well to recall that by trained propensity and tradition the business men, great and small, are after all, each in their degree, lieutenants of those Vested Interests which the projected organization of industry is designed to displace,—schooled in their tactics and marching under their banners. The experience of the war administration and its management of industry by help of the business men during the past few years goes to show what manner of industrial wisdom is to be looked for where capable and well-intentioned business men are called in to direct industry with a view to maximum production and economy. For its responsible personnel the administration has uniformly drawn on experienced business men, preferably men of successful experience in Big Business; that is to say, trained men with a shrewd eye to the main chance. And the tale of its adventures, so far as a businesslike reticence has allowed them to become known, is an amazing comedy of errors; which runs to substantially the same issue whether it is told of one or another of the many departments, boards, councils, commissions, and administrations, that have had this work to do.

Notoriously, this choice of personnel has with singular uniformity proved to be of doubtful advisability, not to choose a harsher epithet. The policies pursued, doubtless with the best and most sagacious intentions of which this businesslike personnel have been capable, have uniformly resulted in the safeguarding of investments and the allocation of commercial profits; all the while that the avowed aim of it all, and doubtless the conscientious purpose of the businesslike administrators, has been quantity production of essential goods. The more that comes to light, the more visible becomes the difference between the avowed purpose and the tangible performance. Tangible performance in the way of productive industry is precisely what the business men do not know how to propose, but it is also that on which the possible success of any projected plan of overturn will always rest. Yet it is also to be remarked that even the reluctant and blindfold endeavors of these businesslike administrators to break away from their life-long rule of reasonable earnings, appear to have resulted in a very appreciably increased industrial output per unit of man power and equipment employed. That such was the outcome under the war administration is presumably due in great part to the fact that the business men in charge were unable to exercise so strict a control over the working force of technicians and skilled operatives during that period of stress.

And here the argument comes in touch with one of the substantial reasons why there need be no present fear of a revolutionary overturn. By settled habit, the American population are quite unable to see their way to entrust any appreciable responsibility to any other than business men; at the same time that such a move of overturn can hope to succeed only if it excludes the business men from all positions of responsibility. This sentimental deference of the American people to the sagacity of its business men is massive, profound, and alert. So much so that it will take harsh and protracted experience to remove it, or to divert it sufficiently for the purpose of any revolutionary diversion. And more particularly, popular sentiment in this country will not tolerate the assumption of responsibility by the technicians, who are in the popular apprehension conceived to be a somewhat fantastic brotherhood of over-specialized cranks, not to be trusted out of sight except under the restraining hand of safe and sane business men. Nor are the technicians themselves in the habit of taking a greatly different view of their own case. They still feel themselves, in the nature of things, to fall into place as employes of those enterprising business men who are, in the nature of things, elected to get something for nothing. Absentee ownership is secure, just yet. In time, with sufficient provocation, this popular frame of mind may change, of course; but it is in any case a matter of an appreciable lapse of time.

Even such a scant and bare outline of generalities as has been hastily sketched above will serve to show that any effectual overturn of the established order is not a matter to be undertaken out of hand, or to be manœuvred into shape by makeshifts after the initial move has been made. There is no chance without deliberate preparations from beforehand. There are two main lines of preparations that will have to be taken care of by any body of men who may contemplate such a move: (a) An inquiry into existing conditions and into the available ways and means; and (b) the setting up of practicable organization tables and a survey of the available personnel. And bound up with this work of preparation, and conditioning it, provision must also be made for the growth of such a spirit of teamwork as will be ready to undertake and undergo this critical adventure. All of which will take time.

It will be necessary to investigate and to set out in a convincing way what are the various kinds and lines of waste that are necessarily involved in the present businesslike control of industry; what are the abiding causes of these wasteful and obstructive practices; and what economies of management and production will become practicable on the elimination of the present businesslike control. This will call for diligent teamwork on the part of a suitable group of economists and engineers, who will have to be drawn together by self-selection on the basis of a common interest in productive efficiency, economical use of resources, and an equitable distribution of the consumable output. Hitherto no such self-selection of competent persons has visibly taken place, and the beginnings of a plan for team-work in carrying on such an inquiry are yet to be made.

In the course of this contemplated inquiry and on the basis afforded by its findings there is no less serious work to be done in the way of deliberation and advisement, among the members of the group in question and in consultation with outside technological men who know what can best be done with the means in hand, and whose interest in things drives them to dip into the same gainless adventure. This will involve the setting up of organization tables to cover the efficient use of the available resources and equipment, as well as to re-organize the traffic involved in the distribution of the output.

By way of an illustrative instance, to show by an example something of what the scope and method of this inquiry and advisement will presumably be like, it may be remarked that under the new order the existing competitive commercial traffic engaged in the distribution of goods to consumers will presumably fall away, in the main, for want of a commercial incentive. It is well known, in a general way, that the present organization of this traffic, by wholesale and retail merchandising, involves a very large and very costly duplication of work, equipment, stock, and personnel,—several hundred per cent. more than would be required by an economically efficient management of the traffic on a reasonable plan. In looking for a way out of the present extremely wasteful merchandising traffic, and in working out organization tables for an equitable and efficient distribution of goods to consumers, the experts in the case will, it is believed, be greatly helped out by detailed information on such existing organizations as, e.g., the distributing system of the Chicago Packers, the chain stores, and the mail-order houses. These are commercial organizations, of course, and as such they are managed with a view to the commercial gain of their owners and managers; but they are at the same time designed to avoid the ordinary wastes of the ordinary retail distribution, for the benefit of their absentee owners. There are not a few object-lessons of economy of this practical character to be found among the Vested Interests; so much so that the economies which result from them are among the valuable capitalized assets of these business concerns.

This contemplated inquiry will, of course, also be useful in the way of publicity; to show, concretely and convincingly, what are the inherent defects of the present businesslike control of industry, why these defects are inseparable from a businesslike control under existing circumstances, and what may fairly be expected of an industrial management which takes no account of absentee ownership. The ways and means of publicity to be employed is a question that plainly cannot profitably be discussed beforehand, so long as the whole question of the contemplated inquiry itself has little more than a speculative interest; and much the same will have to be said as to the scope and detail of the inquiry, which will have to be determined in great part by the interest and qualifications of the men who are to carry it on. Nothing but provisional generalities could at all confidently be sketched into its program until the work is in hand.

The contemplated eventual shift to a new and more practicable system of industrial production and distribution has been here spoken of as a "revolutionary overturn" of the established order. This flagitious form of words is here used chiefly because the Guardians of the established order are plainly apprehensive of something sinister that can be called by no gentler name, rather than with the intention of suggesting that extreme and subversive measures alone can now save the life of the underlying population from the increasingly disserviceable rule of the Vested Interests. The move which is here discussed in a speculative way under this sinister form of words, as a contingency to be guarded against by fair means and foul, need, in effect, be nothing spectacular; assuredly it need involve no clash of arms or fluttering of banners, unless, as is beginning to seem likely, the Guardians of the old order should find that sort of thing expedient. In its elements, the move will be of the simplest and most matter-of-fact character; although there will doubtless be many intricate adjustments to be made in detail. In principle, all that is necessarily involved is a disallowance of absentee ownership; that is to say, the disestablishment of an institution which has, in the course of time and change, proved to be noxious to the common good. The rest will follow quite simply from the cancelment of this outworn and footless vested right.

By absentee ownership, as the term applies in this connection, is here to be understood the ownership of an industrially useful article by any person or persons who are not habitually employed in the industrial use of it. In this connection, office work of a commercial nature is not rated as industrial employment. A corollary of some breadth follows immediately, although it is so obvious an implication of the main proposition that it should scarcely need explicit statement: An owner who is employed in the industrial use of a given parcel of property owned by him, will still be an "absentee owner," within the meaning of the term, in case he is not the only person habitually employed in its use. A further corollary follows, perhaps less obvious at first sight, but no less convincing on closer attention to the sense of the terms employed: Collective ownership, of the corporate form, that is to say ownership by a collectivity instituted *ad hoc*, also falls away as being unavoidably absentee ownership, within the meaning of the term. It will be noted that all this does not touch joint ownership of property held in undivided interest by a household group and made use of by the members of the household conjointly. It is only in so far as the household is possessed of useful property not made use of by its members, or not made use of without hired help, that its ownership of such property falls within the meaning of the term, absentee ownership. To be sufficiently explicit, it may be added that the cancelment of absentee ownership as here understood will apply indiscriminately to all industrially useful objects, whether realty or personalty, whether natural resources, equipment, banking capital, or wrought goods in stock.

As an immediate consequence of this cancelment of absentee ownership it should seem to be altogether probable that industrially useful articles will presently cease to be used for purposes of ownership, that is to say for purposes of private gain; although there might be no administrative interference with such use. Under the existing state of the industrial arts, neither the natural resources drawn on for power and materials nor the equipment employed in the great and controlling industries are of a nature to lend themselves to any other than absentee ownership; and these industries control the situation, so that private enterprise for gain on a small scale would scarcely find a suitable market. At the same time the inducement to private accumulation of wealth at the cost of the community would virtually fall away, inasmuch as the inducement to such accumulation now is in nearly all cases an ambition to come in for something in the way of absentee ownership. In effect, other incentives are a negligible quantity. Evidently, the secondary effects of such cancelment will go far, in more than one direction, but evidently, too, there could be little profit in endeavoring to follow up these ulterior contingencies in extended speculations here.

As to the formalities, of a legal complexion, that would be involved in such a disallowance of absentee ownership, they need also be neither large nor intricate; at least not in their main incidence. It will in all probability take the shape of a cancelment of all corporation securities, as an initial move. Articles of partnership, evidences of debt, and other legal instruments which now give title to property not in hand or not in use by the owner, will be voided by the same act. In all probability this will be sufficient for the purpose.

This act of disallowance may be called subversive and revolutionary; but while there is no intention here to offer anything in the way of exculpation, it is necessary to an objective appraisal of the contemplated move to note that the effect of such disallowance would be subversive or revolutionary only in a figurative sense of the words. It would all of it neither subvert nor derange any substantial mechanical contrivance or relation, nor need it materially disturb the relations, either as workman or as consumer of goods and services, of any appreciable number of persons now engaged in productive industry. In fact, the disallowance will touch nothing more substantial than a legal make-believe. This would, of course, be serious enough in its consequences to those classes—called the kept classes—whose livelihood hangs on the maintenance of this legal make-believe. So, likewise, it would vacate the occupation of the "middleman," which likewise turns on the maintenance of this legal make-believe; which gives "title" to that to which one stands in no material relation.

Doubtless, hardship will follow thick and fast, among those classes who are least inured to privation; and doubtless all men will agree that it is a great pity. But this evil is, after all, a side issue, as regards the present argument, which has to do with nothing else than the practicability of the scheme. So it is necessary to note that, however detrimental to the special interests of the absentee owners this move may be, yet it will not in any degree derange or diminish those material facts that constitute the ways and means of productive industry; nor will it in any degree enfeeble or mutilate that joint stock of technical knowledge and practice that constitutes the intellectual working force of the industrial system. It does not directly touch the material facts of industry, for better or worse. In this sense it is a completely idle matter, in its immediate incidence, whatever its secondary consequences may be believed to be.

But there is no doubt that a proposal to disallow absentee ownership will shock the moral sensibilities of many persons; more particularly the sensibilities of the absentee owners. To avoid the appearance of willful neglect, therefore, it is necessary to speak also of the "moral aspect." There is no intention here to argue the moral merits of this contemplated disallowance of absentee ownership; or to argue for or against such a move, on moral or other grounds. Absentee ownership is legally sound today. Indeed, as is well known, the Constitution includes a clause which specially safeguards its security. If, and when, the law is changed, in this respect, what is so legal today will of course cease to be legal. There is, in fact, not much more to be said about it; except that, in the last resort, the economic moralities wait on the economic necessities. The economic-moral sense of the American community today runs unequivocally to the effect that absentee ownership is fundamentally and eternally right and good; and it should seem reasonable to believe that it will continue to run to that effect for some time yet.

There has lately been some irritation and faultfinding with what is called "profiteering" and there may be more or less uneasy discontent with what is felt to be an unduly disproportionate inequality in the present distribution of income; but apprehensive persons should not lose sight of the main fact that absentee ownership after all is the idol of every true American heart. It is the substance of things hoped for and the reality of things not seen. To achieve (or to inherit) a competency, that is to say to accumulate such wealth as will assure a "decent" livelihood in industrial *absentia*, is the universal, and universally laudable, ambition of all who have reached years of discretion; but it all means the same thing—to get something for nothing, at any cost. Similarly universal is the awestruck deference with which the larger absentee owners are looked up to for guidance and example. These substantial citizens are the ones who have "made good," in the popular apprehension. They are the great and good men whose lives "all remind us we can make our lives sublime, etc."

This commercialized frame of mind is a sturdy outgrowth of many generations of consistent training in the pursuit of the main chance; it is second nature, and there need be no fear that it will allow the Americans to see workday facts in any other than its own perspective, just yet. The most tenacious factor in any civilization is a settled popular frame of mind, and to this abiding American frame of mind absentee ownership is the controlling center of all the economic realities.

• • •

So, having made plain that all this argument on a practicable overturn of the established order has none but a speculative interest, the argument can go on to consider what will be the nature of the initial move of overturn which is to break with the old order of absentee ownership and set up a régime of workmanship governed by the country's technicians.

As has already been called to mind, repeatedly, the effective management of the industrial system at large is already in the hands of the technicians, so far as regards the work actually done; but it is all under the control of the Vested Interests, representing absentee owners, so far as regards its failure to work. And the failure is, quite reasonably, attracting much attention lately. In this two-cleft, or bi-cameral, administration of industry, the technicians may be said to represent the community at large in its industrial capacity, or in other words the industrial system as a going concern; whereas the business men speak for the commercial interest of the absentee owners, as a body which holds the industrial community in usufruct. It is the part of the technicians, between them, to know the country's available resources, in mechanical power and equipment; to know and put in practice the joint stock of technological knowledge which is indispensable to industrial production; as well as to know and take care of the community's habitual need and use of consumable goods. They are, in effect, the general staff of production engineers, under whose surveillance the required output of goods and services is produced and distributed to the consumers. Whereas it is the part of the business men to know what rate and volume of production and distribution will best serve the commercial interest of the absentee owners, and to put this commercial knowledge in practice by nicely limiting production and distribution of the output to such a rate and volume as their commercial traffic will bear—that is to say, what will yield the largest net income to the absentee owners in terms of price. In this work of sagaciously retarding industry the captains of industry necessarily work at cross purposes, among themselves, since the traffic is of a competitive nature.

Accordingly, in this two-cleft arrangement of administrative functions, it is the duty of the technicians to plan the work and to carry it on; and it is the duty of the captains of industry to see that the work will benefit none but the captains and their associated absentee owners, and that it is not pushed beyond the salutary minimum which their commercial traffic will bear. In all that concerns the planning and execution of the work done, the technicians necessarily take the initiative and exercise the necessary creative surveillance and direction; that being what they, and they alone, are good for; whereas the businesslike deputies of the absentee owners sagaciously exercise a running veto power over the technicians and their productive industry. They are able effectually to exercise this commercially sagacious veto power by the fact that the technicians are, in effect, their employes, hired to do their bidding and fired if they do not; and perhaps no less by this other fact, that the technicians have hitherto been working piecemeal, as scattered individuals under their master's eye; they have hitherto not drawn together on their own ground and taken counsel together as a general staff of industry, to determine what had best be done and what not. So that they have hitherto figured in the conduct of the country's industrial enterprise only as a technological extension of the business men's grasp on the commercial main chance.

Yet, immediately and unremittingly, the technicians and their advice and surveillance are essential to any work whatever in those great primary industries on which the country's productive systems turn, and which set the pace for all the rest. And it is obvious that so soon as they shall draw together, in a reasonably inclusive way, and take common counsel as to what had best be done, they are in a position to say what work shall be done and to fix the terms on which it is to be done. In short, so far as regards the technical requirements of the case, the situation is ready for a self-selected, but inclusive, Soviet of technicians to take over the economic affairs of the country and to allow and disallow what they may agree on; provided always that they live within the requirements of that state of the industrial arts whose keepers they are, and provided that their pretensions continue to have the support of the industrial rank and file; which comes near saying that their Soviet must consistently and effectually take care of the material welfare of the underlying population.

Now, this revolutionary posture of the present state of the industrial arts may be undesirable, in some respects, but there is nothing to be gained by denying the fact. So soon—but only so soon—as the engineers draw together, take common counsel, work out a plan of action, and decide to disallow absentee ownership out of hand, that move will have been made. The obvious and simple means of doing it is a conscientious withdrawal of efficiency; that is to say the general strike, to include so much of the country's staff of technicians as will suffice to incapacitate the industrial system at large by their withdrawal, for such time as may be required to enforce their argument.

In its elements, the project is simple and obvious, but its working out will require much painstaking preparation, much more than appears on the face of this bald statement; for it also follows from the present state of the industrial arts and from the character of the industrial system in which modern technology works out, that even a transient failure to make good in the conduct of productive industry will result in a precipitate collapse of the enterprise.

By themselves alone, the technicians can, in a few weeks, effectually incapacitate the country's productive industry sufficiently for the purpose. No one who will dispassionately consider the technical character of this industrial system will fail to recognize that fact. But so long as they have not, at least, the tolerant consent of the population at large, backed by the aggressive support of the trained working force engaged in transportation and in the greater primary industries, they will be substantially helpless to set up a practicable working organization on the new footing; which is the same as saying that they will in that case accomplish nothing more to the purpose than a transient period of hardship and dissension.

Accordingly, if it be presumed that the production engineers are of a mind to play their part, there will be at least two main lines of subsidiary preparation to be taken care of before any overt move can reasonably be undertaken: (a) An extensive campaign of inquiry and publicity, such as will bring the underlying population to a reasonable understanding of what it is all about; and (b) the working-out of a common understanding and a solidarity of sentiment between the technicians and the working force engaged in transportation and in the greater underlying industries of the system: to which is to be added as being nearly indispensable from the outset, an active adherence to this plan on the part of the trained workmen in the great generality of the mechanical industries. Until these prerequisites are taken care of, any project for the overturn of the established order of absentee ownership will be nugatory.

By way of conclusion it may be recalled again that, just yet, the production engineers are a scattering lot of fairly contented subalterns, working piecemeal under orders from the deputies of the absentee owners; the working force of the great mechanical industries, including transportation, are still nearly out of touch and out of sympathy with the technical men, and are bound in rival trade organizations whose sole and self-seeking interest converges on the full dinner-pail; while the underlying population are as nearly uninformed on the state of things as the Guardians of the Vested Interests, including the commercialized newspapers, can manage to keep them, and they are consequently still in a frame of mind to tolerate no substantial abatement of absentee ownership; and the constituted authorities are competently occupied with maintaining the status quo. There is nothing in the situation that should reasonably flutter the sensibilities of the Guardians or of that massive body of well-to-do citizens who make up the rank and file of absentee owners, just yet.

The Socialist Economics of Karl Marx and His Followers

The substance of lectures before students in Harvard University in April, 1906.

The Socialist Economics of Karl Marx and His Followers

I. The Theories of Karl Marx

The system of doctrines worked out by Marx is characterized by a certain boldness of conception and a great logical consistency. Taken in detail, the constituent elements of the system are neither novel nor iconoclastic, nor does Marx at any point claim to have discovered previously hidden facts or to have invented recondite formulations of facts already known; but the system as a whole has an air of originality and initiative such as is rarely met with among the sciences that deal with any phase of human culture. How much of this distinctive character the Marxian system owes to the personal traits of its creator is not easy to say, but what marks it off from all other systems of economic theory is not a matter of personal idiosyncrasy. It differs characteristically from all systems of theory that had preceded it, both in its premises and in its aims. The (hostile) critics of Marx have not sufficiently appreciated the radical character of his departure in both of these respects, and have, therefore, commonly lost themselves in a tangled scrutiny of supposedly abstruse details; whereas those writers who have been in sympathy with his teachings have too commonly been disciples bent on exegesis and on confirming their fellow-disciples in the faith.

Except as a whole and except in the light of its postulates and aims, the Marxian system is not only not tenable, but it is not even intelligible. A discussion of a given isolated feature of the system (such as the theory of value) from the point of view of classical economics (such as that offered by Böhm-Bawerk) is as futile as a discussion of solids in terms of two dimensions.

Neither as regards his postulates and preconceptions nor as regards the aim of his inquiry is Marx's position an altogether single-minded one. In neither respect does his position come of a single line of antecedents. He is of no single school of philosophy, nor are his ideals those of any single group of speculators living before his time. For this reason he takes his place as an originator of a school of thought as well as the leader of a movement looking to a practical end.

As to the motives which drive him and the aspirations which guide him, in destructive criticism and in creative speculation alike, he is primarily a theoretician busied with the analysis of economic phenomena and their organization into a consistent and faithful system of scientific knowledge; but he is, at the same time, consistently and tenaciously alert to the bearing which each step in the progress of his theoretical work has upon the propaganda. His work has, therefore, an air of bias, such as belongs to an advocate's argument; but it is not, therefore, to be assumed, nor indeed to be credited, that his propagandist aims have in any substantial way deflected his inquiry or his speculations from the faithful pursuit of scientific truth. His socialistic bias may color his polemics, but his logical grasp is too neat and firm to admit of any bias, other than that of his metaphysical preconceptions, affecting his theoretical work.

There is no system of economic theory more logical than that of Marx. No member of the system, no single article of doctrine, is fairly to be understood, criticised, or defended except as an articulate member of the whole and in the light of the preconceptions and postulates which afford the point of departure and the controlling norm of the whole. As regards these preconceptions and postulates, Marx draws on two distinct lines of antecedents,—the Materialistic Hegelianism and the English system of Natural Rights. By his earlier training he is an adept in the Hegelian method of speculation and inoculated with the metaphysics of development underlying the Hegelian system. By his later training he is an expert in the system of Natural Rights and Natural Liberty, ingrained in his ideals of life and held inviolate throughout. He does not take a critical attitude toward the underlying principles of Natural Rights. Even his Hegelian preconceptions of development never carry him the length of questioning the fundamental principles of that system. He is only more ruthlessly consistent in working out their content than his natural-rights antagonists in the liberal-classical school. His polemics run against the specific tenets of the liberal school, but they run wholly on the ground afforded by the premises of that school. The ideals of his propaganda are natural-rights ideals, but his theory of the working out of these ideals in the course of history rests on the Hegelian metaphysics of development, and his method of speculation and construction of theory is given by the Hegelian dialectic.

$$\bullet \ \bullet \ \bullet$$

What first and most vividly centred interest on Marx and his speculations was his relation to the revolutionary socialistic movement; and it is those features of his doctrines which bear immediately on the propaganda that still continue to hold the attention of the greater number of his critics. Chief among these doctrines, in the apprehension of his critics, is the theory of value, with its corollaries: (*a*) the doctrines of the exploitation of labor by capital; and (*b*) the laborer's claim to the whole product of his labor. Avowedly, Marx traces his doctrine of labor value to Ricardo, and through him to the classical economists.[1] The laborer's claim to the whole product of labor, which is pretty

---

[1] Cf. *Critique of Political Economy*, chap. i., "Notes on the History of the Theory of Commodities," pp. 56-73 (English translation, New York, 1904).

constantly implied, though not frequently avowed by Marx, he has in all probability taken from English writers of the early nineteenth century,[1] more particularly from William Thompson. These doctrines are, on their face, nothing but a development of the conceptions of natural rights which then pervaded English speculation and afforded the metaphysical ground of the liberal movement. The more formidable critics of the Marxian socialism have made much of these doctrinal elements that further the propaganda, and have, by laying the stress on these, diverted attention from other elements that are of more vital consequence to the system as a body of theory. Their exclusive interest in this side of "scientific socialism" has even led them to deny the Marxian system all substantial originality, and make it a (doubtfully legitimate) offshoot of English Liberalism and natural rights.[2] But this is one-sided criticism. It may hold as against certain tenets of the so-called "scientific socialism," but it is not altogether to the point as regards the Marxian system of theory. Even the Marxian theory of value, surplus value, and exploitation, is not simply the doctrine of William Thompson, transcribed and sophisticated in a forbidding terminology, however great the superficial resemblance and however large Marx's unacknowledged debt to Thompson may be on these heads. For many details and for much of his animus Marx may be indebted to the Utilitarians; but, after all, his system of theory, taken as a whole, lies within the frontiers of neo-Hegelianism, and even the details are worked out in accord with the preconceptions of that school of thought and have taken on the complexion that would properly belong to them on that ground. It is, therefore, not by an itemized scrutiny of the details of doctrine and by tracing their pedigree in detail that a fair conception of Marx and his contribution to economics may be reached, but rather

---

[1] See Menger, *Right to the Whole Produce of Labor*, section iii.-v. and viii.-ix., and Foxwell's admirable Introduction to Menger.
[2] See Menger and Foxwell, as above, and Schaeffle, *Quintessence of Socialism* and *The Impossibility of Social Democracy*.

by following him from his own point of departure out into the ramifications of his theory, and so overlooking the whole in the perspective which the lapse of time now affords us, but which he could not himself attain, since he was too near to his own work to see why he went about it as he did.

• • •

The comprehensive system of Marxism is comprised within the scheme of the Materialistic Conception of History.[1] This materialistic conception is essentially Hegelian,[2] although it belongs with the Hegelian Left, and its immediate affiliation is with Feuerbach, not with the direct line of Hegelian orthodoxy. The chief point of interest here, in identifying the materialistic conception with Hegelianism, is that this identification throws it immediately and uncompromisingly into contrast with Darwinism and the post-Darwinian conceptions of evolution. Even if a plausible English pedigree should be worked out for this Materialistic Conception, or "Scientific Socialism," as has been attempted, it remains none the less true that the conception with which Marx went to his work was a transmuted framework of Hegelian dialectic.[3]

Roughly, Hegelian materialism differs from Hegelian orthodoxy by inverting the main logical sequence, not by discarding the logic or resorting to new tests of truth or finality. One might say, though perhaps with excessive crudity, that, where Hegel pronounces his dictum, *Das Denken ist das Sein*, the materialists, particularly Marx and Engels, would say *Das Sein macht das Denken*. But in both cases some sort of a creative primacy is

---

[1] See Engels, *The Development of Socialism from Utopia to Science*, especially section ii. and the opening paragraphs of section iii.; also the preface of *Zur Kritik der politischen Oekonomie*.

[2] See Engels, as above, and also his *Feuerbach: The Roots of Socialist Philosophy* (translation, Chicago, Kerr & Co., 1903).

[3] See, *e.g.*, Seligman, *The Economic Interpretation of History*, Part I.

assigned to one or the other member of the complex, and in neither case is the relation between the two members a causal relation. In the materialistic conception man's spiritual life—what man thinks—is a reflex of what he is in the material respect, very much in the same fashion as the orthodox Hegelian would make the material world a reflex of the spirit. In both the dominant norm of speculation and formulation of theory is the conception of movement, development, evolution, progress; and in both the movement is conceived necessarily to take place by the method of conflict or struggle. The movement is of the nature of progress,—gradual advance towards a goal, toward the realization in explicit form of all that is implicit in the substantial activity involved in the movement. The movement is, further, self-conditioned and self-acting: it is an unfolding by inner necessity. The struggle which constitutes the method of movement or evolution is, in the Hegelian system proper, the struggle of the spirit for self-realization by the process of the well-known three-phase dialectic. In the materialistic conception of history this dialectical movement becomes the class struggle of the Marxian system.

The class struggle is conceived to be "material," but the term "material" is in this connection used in a metaphorical sense. It does not mean mechanical or physical, or even physiological, but economic. It is material in the sense that it is a struggle between classes for the material means of life. "The materialistic conception of history proceeds on the principle that production and, next to production, the exchange of its products is the groundwork of every social order."[1] The social order takes its form through the class struggle, and the character of the class struggle at any given phase of the unfolding development of society is determined by "the prevailing mode of economic production and exchange." The dialectic of the movement of social progress, therefore, moves on the spiritual plane of human desire and passion, not on the (literally) material plane of mechanical

---

[1] Engels, *Development of Socialism*, beginning of section iii.

and physiological stress, on which the developmental process of brute creation unfolds itself. It is a sublimated materialism; sublimated by the dominating presence of the conscious human spirit; but it is conditioned by the material facts of the production of the means of life.[1] The ultimately active forces involved in the process of unfolding social life are (apparently) the material agencies engaged in the mechanics of production; but the dialectic of the process—the class struggle—runs its course only among and in terms of the secondary (epigenetic) forces of human consciousness engaged in the valuation of the material products of industry. A consistently materialistic conception, consistently adhering to a materialistic interpretation of the process of development as well as of the facts involved in the process, could scarcely avoid making its putative dialectic struggle a mere unconscious and irrelevant conflict of the brute material forces. This would have amounted to an interpretation in terms of opaque cause and effect, without recourse to the concept of a conscious class struggle, and it might have led to a concept of evolution similar to the unteleological Darwinian concept of natural selection. It could scarcely have led to the Marxian notion of a conscious class struggle as the one necessary method of social progress, though it might conceivably, by the aid of empirical generalization, have led to a scheme of social process in which a class struggle would be included as an incidental though perhaps highly efficient factor.[2] It would have led, as Darwinism has, to a concept of a process of cumulative change in social structure and function; but this process, being essentially a cumulative sequence of causation, opaque and unteleological, could not, without an infusion of pious fancy by the speculator, be asserted to involve progress as distinct from retrogression or to tend to a

---

[1] *Cf.*, on this point, Max Adler, "Kausalität und Teleologie im Streite um die Wissenschaft" (included in *Marx—Studien*, edited by Adler and Hilfendirg, vol. i.), particularly section xi.; *cf.* also Ludwig Stein, *Die soziale Frage im Lichte der Philosophie*, whom Adler criticizes and claims to have refuted.
[2] *Cf.*, Adler as above.

"realization" or "self-realization" of the human spirit or of anything else. Neither could it conceivably be asserted to lead up to a final term, a goal to which all lines of the process should converge and beyond which the process would not go, such as the assumed goal of the Marxian process of class struggle which is conceived to cease in the classless economic structure of the socialistic final term. In Darwinianism there is no such final or perfect term, and no definitive equilibrium.

The disparity between Marxism and Darwinism, as well as the disparity within the Marxian system between the range of material facts that are conceived to be the fundamental forces of the process, on the one hand, and the range of spiritual facts within which the dialectic movement proceeds,—this disparity is shown in the character assigned the class struggle by Marx and Engels. The struggle is asserted to be a conscious one, and proceeds on a recognition by the competing classes of their mutually incompatible interests with regard to the material means of life. The class struggle proceeds on motives of interest, and a recognition of class interest can, of course, be reached only by reflection on the facts of the case. There is, therefore, not even a direct causal connection between the material forces in the case and the choice of a given interested line of conduct. The attitude of the interested party does not result from the material forces so immediately as to place it within the relation of direct cause and effect, nor even with such a degree of intimacy as to admit of its being classed as a tropismatic, or even instinctive, response to the impact of the material force in question. The sequence of reflection, and the consequent choice of sides to a quarrel, run entirely alongside of the range of material facts concerned.

A further characteristic of the doctrine of class struggle requires mention. While the concept is not Darwinian, it is also not legitimately Hegelian, whether of the Right or the Left. It is of a utilitarian origin and of English pedigree, and it belongs to Marx by virtue of his having borrowed its elements from the system of self-interest. It is in fact a piece of hedonism, and is related to Bentham rather than to Hegel. It proceeds on the grounds of the hedonistic calculus, which is equally foreign to the Hegelian notion of an unfolding process and to the post-Darwinian notions of cumulative causation. As regards the tenability of the doctrine, apart from the question of its derivation and its compatibility with the neo-Hegelian postulates, it is to be added that it is quite out of harmony with the later results of psychological inquiry,—just as is true of the use made of the hedonistic calculus by the classical (Austrian) economics.

• • •

Within the domain covered by the materialistic conception, that is to say within the domain of unfolding human culture, which is the field of Marxian speculation at large, Marx has more particularly devoted his efforts to an analysis and theoretical formulation of the present situation,—the current phase of the process, the capitalistic system. And, since the prevailing mode of the production of goods determines the institutional, intellectual, and spiritual life of the epoch, by determining the form and method of the current class struggle, the discussion necessarily begins with the theory of "capitalistic production," or production as carried on under the capitalistic system.[1] Under the capitalistic system, that is to say under the system of modern

---

[1] It may be noted, by way of caution to readers familiar with the terms only as employed by the classical (English and Austrian) economists, that in Marxian usage "capitalistic production" means production of goods for the market by hired labor under the direction of employers who own (or control) the means of production and are engaged in industry for the sake of a profit. "Capital" is wealth (primarily funds) so employed. In these and other related points of terminological usage Marx is, of course, much more closely in touch with colloquial usage than those economists of the classical line who make capital signify "the products of past industry used as aids to further production." With Marx "Capitalism" implies certain relations of ownership, no less than the "productive use" which is alone insisted on by so many later economists in defining the term.

business traffic, production is a production of commodities, merchantable goods, with a view to the price to be obtained for them in the market. The great fact on which all industry under this system hinges is the price of marketable goods. Therefore it is at this point that Marx strikes into the system of capitalistic production, and therefore the theory of value becomes the dominant feature of his economics and the point of departure for the whole analysis, in all its voluminous ramifications.[1]

It is scarcely worth while to question what serves as the beginning of wisdom in the current criticisms of Marx; namely, that he offers no adequate proof of his labor-value theory.[2] It is even safe to go farther, and say that he offers no proof of it. The feint which occupies the opening paragraphs of the *Kapital* and the corresponding passages of *Zur Kritik*, etc., is not to be taken seriously as an attempt to prove his position on this head by the ordinary recourse to argument. It is rather a self-satisfied superior's playful mystification of those readers (critics) whose limited powers do not enable them to see that his proposition is self-evident. Taken on the Hegelian (neo-Hegelian) ground, and seen in the light of the general materialistic conception, the proposition that value = labor-cost is self-evident, not to say tautological. Seen in any other light, it has no particular force.

In the Hegelian scheme of things the only substantial reality

---

[1] In the sense that the theory of value affords the point of departure and the fundamental concepts out of which the further theory of the workings of capitalism is constructed,—in this sense, and in this sense only, is the theory of value the central doctrine and the critical tenet of Marxism. It does not follow that the Marxist doctrine of an irresistible drift towards a socialistic consummation hangs on the defensibility of the labor-value theory, nor even that the general structure of the Marxist economics would collapse if translated into other terms than those of this doctrine of labor value. *Cf.* Böhm-Bawerk, *Karl Marx and the Close of his System*; and, on the other hand, Franz Oppenheimer, *Das Grundgesetz der Marx'schen Gesellschaftslehre*, and Rudolf Goldscheid, *Verelendungs- oder Meliorationstheorie.*

[2] *Cf.*, *e.g.*, Böhm-Bawerk, as above; Georg Adler, *Grundlagen der Karl Marx'schen Kritik.*

is the unfolding life of the spirit. In the neo-Hegelian scheme, as embodied in the materialistic conception, this reality is translated into terms of the unfolding (material) life of man in society.[1] In so far as the goods are products of industry, they are the output of this unfolding life of man, a material residue embodying a given fraction of this forceful life process. In this life process lies all substantial reality, and all finally valid relations of quantivalence between the products of this life process must run in its terms. The life process, which, when it takes the specific form of an expenditure of labor power, goes to produce goods, is a process of material forces, the spiritual or mental features of the life process and of labor being only its insubstantial reflex. It is consequently only in the material changes wrought by this expenditure of labor power that the metaphysical substance of life—labor power—can be embodied; but in these changes of material fact it cannot but be embodied, since these are the end to which it is directed.

This balance between goods in respect of their magnitude as output of human labor holds good indefeasibly, in point of the metaphysical reality of the life process, whatever superficial (phenomenal) variations from this norm may occur in men's dealings with the goods under the stress of the strategy of self-interest. Such is the value of the goods in reality; they are equivalents of one another in the proportion in which they partake of this substantial quality, although their true ratio of equivalence may never come to an adequate expression in the transactions involved in the distribution of the goods. This real or true value

---

[1] In much the same way, and with an analogous effect on their theoretical work, in the preconceptions of the classical (including the Austrian) economists, the balance of pleasure and pain is taken to be the ultimate reality in terms of which all economic theory must be stated and to terms of which all phenomena should finally be reduced in any definitive analysis of economic life. It is not the present purpose to inquire whether the one of these uncritical assumptions is in any degree more meritorious or more serviceable than the other.

of the goods is a fact of production, and holds true under all systems and methods of production, whereas the exchange value (the "phenomenal form" of the real value) is a fact of distribution, and expresses the real value more or less adequately according as the scheme of distribution in force at the given time conforms more or less closely to the equities given by production. If the output of industry were distributed to the productive agents strictly in proportion to their shares in production, the exchange value of the goods would be presumed to conform to their real value. But, under the current, capitalistic system, distribution is not in any sensible degree based on the equities of production, and the exchange value of goods under this system can therefore express their real value only with a very rough, and in the main fortuitous, approximation. Under a socialistic régime, where the laborer would get the full product of his labor, or where the whole system of ownership, and consequently the system of distribution, would lapse, values would reach a true expression, if any.

Under the capitalistic system the determination of exchange value is a matter of competitive profit-making, and exchange values therefore depart erratically and incontinently from the proportions that would legitimately be given them by the real values whose only expression they are. Marx's critics commonly identify the concept of "value" with that of "exchange value,"[1] and show that the theory of "value" does not square with the run of the facts of price under the existing system of distribution, piously hoping thereby to have refuted the Marxian doctrine; whereas, of course, they have for the most part not touched it. The misapprehension of the critics may be due to a (possibly intentional) oracular obscurity on the part of Marx. Whether by his fault or their own, their refutations have hitherto been quite

---

[1] Böhm-Bawerk, *Capital and Interest*, Book VI., chap. iii.; also *Karl Marx and the Close of his System*, particularly chap. iv.; Adler, *Grundlagen*, chaps. ii. and iii.

inconclusive. Marx's severest stricture on the iniquities of the capitalistic system is that contained by implication in his development of the manner in which actual exchange value of goods systematically diverges from their real (labor-cost) value. Herein, indeed, lies not only the inherent iniquity of the existing system, but also its fateful infirmity, according to Marx.

The theory of value, then, is *contained in* the main postulates of the Marxian system rather than derived from them. Marx identifies this doctrine, in its elements, with the labor-value theory of Ricardo,[1] but the relationship between the two is that of a superficial coincidence in their main propositions rather than a substantial identity of theoretic contents. In Ricardo's theory the source and measure of value is sought in the effort and sacrifice undergone by the producer, consistently, on the whole, with the Benthamite-utilitarian position to which Ricardo somewhat loosely and uncritically adhered. The decisive fact about labor, that quality by virtue of which it is assumed to be the final term in the theory of production, is its irksomeness. Such is of course not the case in the labor-value theory of Marx, to whom the question of the irksomeness of labor is quite irrelevant, so far as regards the relation between labor and production. The substantial diversity or incompatibility of the two theories shows itself directly when each is employed by its creator in the further analysis of economic phenomena. Since with Ricardo the crucial point is the degree of irksomeness of labor, which serves as a measure both of the labor expended and the value produced, and since in Ricardo's utilitarian philosophy there is no more vital fact underlying this irksomeness, therefore no surplus-value theory follows from the main position. The productiveness of labor is not cumulative, in its own working; and

---

[1] *Cf. Kapital*, vol. i., chap. xv. p. 486 (4th ed.). See also notes 9 and 16 to chap. i. of the same volume, where Marx discusses the labor-value doctrines of Adam Smith and an earlier (anonymous) English writer and compares them with his own. Similar comparisons with the early—classical—value theories recur from time to time in the later portions of *Kapital*.

the Ricardian economics goes on to seek the cumulative productiveness of industry in the functioning of the products of labor when employed in further production and in the irksomeness of the capitalist's abstinence. From which duly follows the general position of classical economics on the theory of production.

With Marx, on the other hand, the labor power expended in production being itself a product and having a substantial value corresponding to its own labor cost, the value of the labor power expended and the value of the product created by its expenditure need not be the same. They are not the same, by supposition, as they would be in any hedonistic interpretation of the facts. Hence a discrepancy arises between the value of the labor power expended in production and the value of the product created, and this discrepancy is covered by the concept of surplus value. Under the capitalistic system, wages being the value (price) of the labor power consumed in industry, it follows that the surplus product of their labor cannot go to the laborers, but becomes the profits of capital and the source of its accumulation and increase. From the fact that wages are measured by the value of labor power rather than by the (greater) value of the product of labor, it follows also that the laborers are unable to buy the whole product of their labor, and so that the capitalists are unable to sell the whole product of industry continuously at its full value, whence arise difficulties of the gravest nature in the capitalistic system, in the way of overproduction and the like.

But the gravest outcome of this systematic discrepancy between the value of labor power and the value of its product is the accumulation of capital out of unpaid labor and the effect of this accumulation on the laboring population. The law of accumulation, with its corollary, the doctrine of the industrial reserve army, is the final term and the objective point of Marx's theory of capitalist production, just as the theory of labor value is his point of departure.[1] While the theory of value and surplus

---

[1] Oppenheimer (*Das Grundgesetz der Marx'schen Gesellschaftslehre*) is right

value are Marx's explanation of the possibility of existence of the capitalistic system, the law of the accumulation of capital is his exposition of the causes which must lead to the collapse of that system and of the manner in which the collapse will come. And since Marx is, always and everywhere, a socialist agitator as well as a theoretical economist, it may be said without hesitation that the law of accumulation is the climax of his great work, from whatever point of view it is looked at, whether as an economic theorem or as a tenet of socialistic doctrine.

The law of capitalistic accumulation may be paraphrased as follows:[1] Wages being the (approximately exact) value of the labor power bought in the wage contract; the price of the product being the (similarly approximate) value of the goods produced; and since the value of the product exceeds that of the labor power by a given amount (surplus value), which by force of the wage contract passes into the possession of the capitalist and is by him in part laid by as savings and added to the capital already in hand, it follows (*a*) that, other things equal, the larger the surplus value, the more rapid the increase of capital; and, also (*b*), that the greater the increase of capital relatively to the labor force employed, the more productive the labor employed and the larger the surplus product available for accumulation. The process of accumulation, therefore, is evidently a cumulative one; and, also evidently, the increase added to capital is an unearned increment drawn from the unpaid surplus product of labor.

But with an appreciable increase of the aggregate capital a change takes place in its technological composition, whereby the "constant" capital (equipment and raw materials) increases

---

in making the theory of accumulation the central element in the doctrines of Marxist socialism, but it does not follow, as Oppenheimer contends, that this doctrine is the keystone of Marx's economic theories. It follows logically from the theory of surplus value, as indicated above, and rests on that theory in such a way that it would fail (in the form in which it is held by Marx) with the failure of the doctrine of surplus value.

[1] See *Kapital*, vol. i., chap. xxiii.

disproportionately as compared with the "variable" capital (wages fund). "Labor-saving devices" are used to a greater extent than before, and labor is saved. A larger proportion of the expenses of production goes for the purchase of equipment and raw materials, and a smaller proportion—though perhaps an absolutely increased amount—goes for the purchase of labor power. Less labor is needed relatively to the aggregate capital employed as well as relatively to the quantity of goods produced. Hence some portion of the increasing labor supply will not be wanted, and an "industrial reserve army," a "surplus labor population," an army of unemployed, comes into existence. This reserve grows relatively larger as the accumulation of capital proceeds and as technological improvements consequently gain ground; so that there result two divergent cumulative changes in the situation,— antagonistic, but due to the same set of forces and, therefore, inseparable: capital increases, and the number of unemployed laborers (relatively) increases also.

This divergence between the amount of capital and output, on the one hand, and the amount received by laborers as wages, on the other hand, has an incidental consequence of some importance. The purchasing power of the laborers, represented by their wages, being the largest part of the demand for consumable goods, and being at the same time, in the nature of the case, progressively less adequate for the purchase of the product, represented by the price of the goods produced, it follows that the market is progressively more subject to glut from overproduction, and hence to commercial crises and depression. It has been argued, as if it were a direct inference from Marx's position, that this maladjustment between production and markets, due to the laborer not getting the full product of his labor, leads directly to the breakdown of the capitalistic system, and so by its own force will bring on the socialistic consummation. Such is not Marx's position, however, although crises and depression play an important part in the course of development that is to lead up to socialism. In Marx's theory, socialism is to come by way of a conscious class movement on the part of the propertyless laborers, who will act advisedly on their own interest and force the revolutionary movement for their own gain. But crises and depression will have a large share in bringing the laborers to a frame of mind suitable for such a move.

Given a growing aggregate capital, as indicated above, and a concomitant reserve of unemployed laborers growing at a still higher rate, as is involved in Marx's position, this body of unemployed labor can be, and will be, used by the capitalists to depress wages, in order to increase profits. Logically, it follows that, the farther and faster capital accumulates, the larger will be the reserve of unemployed, both absolutely and relatively to the work to be done, and the more severe will be the pressure acting to reduce wages and lower the standard of living, and the deeper will be the degradation and misery of the working class and the more precipitately will their condition decline to a still lower depth. Every period of depression, with its increased body of unemployed labor seeking work, will act to hasten and accentuate the depression of wages, until there is no warrant even for holding that wages will, on an average, be kept up to the subsistence minimum.[1] Marx, indeed, is explicit to the effect that such will be the case,—that wages will decline below the subsistence minimum; and he cites English conditions of child labor, misery, and degeneration to substantiate his views.[2] When this has gone far enough, when capitalist production comes near enough to occupying the whole field of industry and has depressed the condition of its laborers sufficiently to make them an effective majority of the community with nothing to lose, then, having taken advice together, they will move, by legal or extra-legal means, by absorbing the state or by subverting it, to establish the social revolution.

---

[1] The "subsistence minimum" is here taken in the sense used by Marx and the classical economists, as meaning what is necessary to keep up the supply of labor at its current rate of efficiency.

[2] See *Kapital*, vol. i., chap. xxiii., sections 4 and 5.

Socialism is to come through class antagonism due to the absence of all property interests from the laboring class, coupled with a generally prevalent misery so profound as to involve some degree of physical degeneration. This misery is to be brought about by the heightened productivity of labor due to an increased accumulation of capital and large improvements in the industrial arts; which in turn is caused by the fact that under a system of private enterprise with hired labor the laborer does not get the whole product of his labor; which, again, is only saying in other words that private ownership of capital goods enables the capitalist to appropriate and accumulate the surplus product of labor. As to what the régime is to be which the social revolution will bring in, Marx has nothing particular to say beyond the general thesis that there will be no private ownership, at least not of the means of production.

• • •

Such are the outlines of the Marxian system of socialism. In all that has been said so far no recourse is had to the second and third volumes of *Kapital*. Nor is it necessary to resort to these two volumes for the general theory of socialism. They add nothing essential, although many of the details of the processes concerned in the working out of the capitalist scheme are treated with greater fulness, and the analysis is carried out with great consistency and with admirable results. For economic theory at large these further two volumes are important enough, but an inquiry into their contents in that connection is not called for here.

Nothing much need be said as to the tenability of this theory. In its essentials, or at least in its characteristic elements, it has for the most part been given up by latter-day socialist writers. The number of those who hold to it without essential deviation is growing gradually smaller. Such is necessarily the case, and for more than one reason. The facts are not bearing it out on certain critical points, such as the doctrine of increasing misery; and the Hegelian philosophical postulates, without which the Marxism of Marx is groundless, are for the most part forgotten by the dogmatists of to-day. Darwinism has largely supplanted Hegelianism in their habits of thought.

The particular point at which the theory is most fragile, considered simply as a theory of social growth, is its implied doctrine of population,—implied in the doctrine of a growing reserve of unemployed workmen. The doctrine of the reserve of unemployed labor involves as a postulate that population will increase anyway, without reference to current or prospective means of life. The empirical facts give at least a very persuasive apparent support to the view expressed by Marx, that misery is, or has hitherto been, no hindrance to the propagation of the race; but they afford no conclusive evidence in support of a thesis to the effect that the number of laborers must increase independently of an increase of the means of life. No one since Darwin would have the hardihood to say that the increase of the human species is not conditioned by the means of living.

But all that does not really touch Marx's position. To Marx, the neo-Hegelian, history, including the economic development, is the life-history of the human species; and the main fact in this life-history, particularly in the economic aspect of it, is the growing volume of human life. This, in a manner of speaking, is the base-line of the whole analysis of the process of economic life, including the phase of capitalist production with the rest. The growth of population is the first principle, the most substantial, most material factor in this process of economic life, so long as it is a process of growth, of unfolding, of exfoliation, and not a phase of decrepitude and decay. Had Marx found that his analysis led him to a view adverse to this position, he would logically have held that the capitalist system is the mortal agony of the race and the manner of its taking off. Such a conclusion is precluded by his Hegelian point of departure, according to which the goal of the life-history of the race in a large way controls the course of that life-history in all its phases, including the phase of capitalism. This goal or end, which controls the process of human development, is the complete realization of life in all its fulness, and the realization is to be reached by a process analogous to the three-phase dialectic, of thesis, antithesis, and synthesis, into which scheme the capitalist system, with its overflowing measure of misery and degradation, fits as the last and most dreadful phase of antithesis. Marx, as a Hegelian,—that is to say, a romantic philosopher,—is necessarily an optimist, and the evil (antithetical element) in life is to him a logically necessary evil, as the antithesis is a necessary phase of the dialectic; and it is a means to the consummation, as the antithesis is a means to the synthesis.

Thorstein Veblen.

University of Chicago.

The Socialist Economics of Karl Marx and His Followers

II. The Later Marxism

Marx worked out his system of theory in the main during the third quarter of the nineteenth century. He came to the work from the standpoint given him by his early training in German thought, such as the most advanced and aggressive German thinking was thru the middle period of the century, and he added to this German standpoint the further premises given him by an exceptionally close contact with and alert observation of the English situation. The result is that he brings to his theoretical work a twofold line of premises, or rather of preconceptions. By early training he is a neo-Hegelian, and from this German source he derives his peculiar formulation of the Materialistic Theory of History. By later experience he acquired the point of view of that Liberal-Utilitarian school which dominated English thought thru the greater part of his active life. To this experience he owes (probably) the somewhat pronounced individualistic preconceptions on which the doctrines of the Full Product of Labor and the Exploitation of Labor are based. These two not altogether compatible lines of doctrine found their way together into the tenets of scientific[1] socialism, and give its characteristic Marxian features to the body of socialist economics.

---

[1] "Scientific" is here used in the half technical sense which by usage it often has in this connection, designating the theories of Marx and his followers.

The socialism that inspires hopes and fears to-day is of the school of Marx. No one is seriously apprehensive of any other so-called socialistic movement, and no one is seriously concerned to criticise or refute the doctrines set forth by any other school of "socialists." It may be that the socialists of the Marxist observance are not always or at all points in consonance with the best accepted body of Marxist doctrine. Those who make up the body of the movement may not always be familiar with the details—perhaps not even with the general features—of the Marxian scheme of economics; but with such consistency as may fairly be looked for in any popular movements the socialists of all countries gravitate toward the theoretical position of the avowed Marxism. In proportion as the movement in any given community grows in mass, maturity, and conscious purpose, it unavoidably takes on a more consistently Marxian complexion. It is not the Marxism of Marx, but the materialism of Darwin, which the socialists of to-day have adopted. The Marxist socialists of Germany have the lead, and the socialists of other countries largely take their cue from the German leaders.

The authentic spokesmen of the current international socialism are avowed Marxists. Exceptions to that rule are very few. On the whole, the substantial truth of the Marxist doctrines is not seriously questioned within the lines of the socialists, tho there may be some appreciable divergence as to what the true Marxist position is on one point and another. Much and eager controversy circles about questions of that class.

The keepers of the socialist doctrines are passably agreed as to the main position and the general principles. Indeed, so secure is this current agreement on the general principles that a very lively controversy on matters of detail may go on without risk of disturbing the general position. This general position is avowedly Marxism. But it is not precisely the position held by Karl Marx. It has been modernized, adapted, filled out, in response to exigencies of a later date than those which conditioned the original formulation of the theories. It is, of course, not admitted by the followers of Marx that any substantial change or departure from the original position has taken place. They are somewhat jealously orthodox, and are impatient of any suggested "improvements" on the Marxist position, as witness the heat engendered in the "revisionist" controversy of a few years back. But the jealous protests of the followers of Marx do not alter the fact that Marxism has undergone some substantial change since it left the hands of its creator. Now and then a more or less consistent disciple of Marx will avow a need of adapting the received doctrines to circumstances that have arisen later than the formulation of the doctrines; and amendments, qualifications, and extensions, with this need in view, have been offered from time to time. But more pervasive tho unavowed changes have come in the teachings of Marxism by way of interpretation and an unintended shifting of the point of view. Virtually, the whole of the younger generation of socialist writers shows such a growth. A citation of personal instances would be quite futile.

• • •

It is the testimony of his friends as well as of his writings that the theoretical position of Marx, both as regards his standpoint and as regards his main tenets, fell into a definitive shape relatively early, and that his later work was substantially a working out of what was contained in the position taken at the outset of his career.[1] By the latter half of the forties, if not by the middle of

---

[1] There is, indeed, a remarkable consistency, amounting substantially to an invariability of position, in Marx's writing, from the *Communist Manifesto* to the last volume of the *Capital*. The only portion of the great *Manifesto* which became antiquated, in the apprehension of its creators, is the polemics addressed to the "Philosophical" socialists of the forties and the illustrative material taken from contemporary politics. The main position and the more important articles of theory—the materialistic conception, the doctrine of class struggle, the theory of value and surplus value, of increasing distress, of the reserve army, of the capitalistic collapse—are to be found in the *Critique of Political Economy* (1859), and much of them in the *Misery of Philosophy*

the forties, Marx and Engels had found the outlook on human life which came to serve as the point of departure and the guide for their subsequent development of theory. Such is the view of the matter expressed by Engels during the latter years of his life.[1] The position taken by the two greater leaders, and held by them substantially intact, was a variant of neo-Hegelianism, as has been indicated in an earlier section of this paper.[2] But neo-Hegelianism was short-lived, particularly considered as a standpoint for scientific theory. The whole romantic school of thought, comprising neo-Hegelianism with the rest, began to go to pieces very soon after it had reached an approach to maturity, and its disintegration proceeded with exceptional speed, so that the close of the third quarter of the century saw the virtual end of it as a vital factor in the development of human knowledge. In the realm of theory, primarily of course in the material sciences, the new era belongs not to romantic philosophy, but to the evolutionists of the school of Darwin. Some few great figures, of course, stood over from the earlier days, but it turns out in the sequel that they have served mainly to mark the rate and degree in which the method of scientific knowledge has left them behind. Such were Virchow and Max Müller, and such, in economic science, were the great figures of the Historical School, and such, in a degree, were also Marx and Engels. The later generation of socialists, the spokesmen and adherents of Marxism during the closing quarter of the century, belong to the new generation, and see the phenomena of human life under the new light. The materialistic

---

(1847), together with the masterful method of analysis and construction which he employed thruout his theoretical work.

[1] *Cf.* Engels, *Feuerbach* (English translation, Chicago, 1903), especially Part IV., and various papers published in the *Neue Zeit*; also the preface to the *Communist Manifesto* written in 1888; also the preface to volume ii. of *Capital*, where Engels argues the question of Marx's priority in connection with the leading theoretical principles of his system.

[2] Cf. *Feuerbach*, as above; *The Development of Socialism from Utopia to Science*, especially sections II. and III.

conception in their handling of it takes on the color of the time in which they lived, even while they retain the phraseology of the generation that went before them.[1]

The difference between the romantic school of thought, to which Marx belonged, and the school of the evolutionists into whose hands the system has fallen,—or perhaps, better, is falling,—is great and pervading, tho it may not show a staring superficial difference at any one point,—at least not yet. The discrepancy between the two is likely to appear more palpable and more sweeping when the new method of knowledge has been applied with fuller realization of its reach and its requirements in that domain of knowledge that once belonged to the neo-Hegelian Marxism. The supplanting of the one by the other has been taking place slowly, gently, in large measure unavowedly, by a sort of precession of the point of view from which men size up the facts and reduce them to intelligible order.

The neo-Hegelian, romantic, Marxian standpoint was wholly personal, whereas the evolutionistic—it may be called Darwinian—standpoint is wholly impersonal. The continuity sought in the facts of observation and imputed to them by the earlier school of theory was a continuity of a personal kind,—a

---

[1] Such a socialist as Anton Menger, *e.g.*, comes into the neo-Marxian school from without, from the field of modern scientific inquiry, and shows, at least virtually, no Hegelian color, whether in the scope of his inquiry, in his method, or in the theoretical work which he puts forth. It should be added that his *Neue Staatslehre* and *Neue Sittenlehre* are the first socialistic constructive work of substantial value as a contribution to knowledge, outside of economic theory proper, that has appeared since Lassalle. The efforts of Engels (*Ursprung der Familie*) and Bebel (*Die Frau*) would scarcely be taken seriously as scientific monographs even by hot-headed socialists if it were not for the lack of anything better. Menger's work is not Marxism, whereas Engels' and Bebel's work of this class is practically without value or originality. The unfitness of the Marxian postulates and methods for the purposes of modern science shows itself in the sweeping barrenness of socialistic literature all along that line of inquiry into the evolution of institutions for the promotion of which the materialistic dialectic was invented.

continuity of reason and consequently of logic. The facts were construed to take such a course as could be established by an appeal to reason between intelligent and fair-minded men. They were supposed to fall into a sequence of logical consistency. The romantic (Marxian) sequence of theory is essentially an intellectual sequence, and it is therefore of a teleological character. The logical trend of it can be argued out. That is to say, it tends to a goal. It must eventuate in a consummation, a final term. On the other hand, in the Darwinian scheme of thought, the continuity sought in and imputed to the facts is a continuity of cause and effect. It is a scheme of blindly cumulative causation, in which there is no trend, no final term, no consummation. The sequence is controlled by nothing but the *vis a tergo* of brute causation, and is essentially mechanical. The neo-Hegelian (Marxian) scheme of development is drawn in the image of the struggling ambitious human spirit: that of Darwinian evolution is of the nature of a mechanical process.[1]

What difference, now, does it make if the materialistic conception is translated from the romantic concepts of Marx into the mechanical concepts of Darwinism? It distorts every feature of the system in some degree, and throws a shadow of doubt on every conclusion that once seemed secure.[2] The first

---

[1] This contrast holds between the original Marxism of Marx and the scope and method of modern science; but it does not, therefore, hold between the latter-day Marxists—who are largely imbued with post-Darwinian concepts—and the non-Marxian scientists. Even Engels, in his latter-day formulation of Marxism, is strongly affected with the notions of post-Darwinian science, and reads Darwinism into Hegel and Marx with a good deal of *naïveté*. (See his *Feuerbach*, especially pp. 93-98 of the English translation.) So, also, the serious but scarcely quite consistent qualifications of the materialistic conception offered by Engels in the letters printed in the *Sozialistische Akademiker*, 1895.

[2] The fact that the theoretical structures of Marx collapse when their elements are converted into the terms of modern science should of itself be sufficient proof that those structures were not built by their maker out of such elements as modern science habitually makes use of. Marx was neither

principle of the Marxian scheme is the concept covered by the term "Materialistic," to the effect that the exigencies of the material means of life control the conduct of men in society thruout, and thereby indefeasibly guide the growth of institutions and shape every shifting trait of human culture. This control of the life of society by the material exigencies takes effect thru men's taking thought of material (economic) advantages and disadvantages, and choosing that which will yield the fuller material measure of life. When the materialistic conception passes under the Darwinian norm, of cumulative causation, it happens, first, that this initial principle itself is reduced to the rank of a habit of thought induced in the speculator who depends on its light by the circumstances of his life, in the way of hereditary bent, occupation, tradition, education, climate, food supply, and the like. But under the Darwinian norm the question of whether and how far material exigencies control human conduct and cultural growth becomes a question of the share which these material exigencies have in shaping men's habits of thought; *i.e.*, their ideals and aspirations, their sense of the true, the beautiful, and the good. Whether and how far these traits of human culture and the institutional structure built out of them are the outgrowth of material (economic) exigencies becomes a question of what kind and degree of efficiency belongs to the economic exigencies among the complex of circumstances that conduce to the formation of habits. It is no longer a question of whether material exigencies rationally should guide men's conduct, but whether, as a matter of brute causation, they do induce such habits of thought in men as the economic interpretation presumes, and whether in the last analysis economic exigencies alone are, directly or indirectly, effective in shaping human habits of thought.

Tentatively and by way of approximation some such

---

ignorant, imbecile, nor disingenuous, and his work must be construed from such a point of view and in terms of such elements as will enable his results to stand substantially sound and convincing.

formulation as that outlined in the last paragraph is apparently what Bernstein and others of the "revisionists" have been seeking in certain of their speculations,[1] and, sitting austere and sufficient on a dry shoal up stream, Kautsky has uncomprehendingly been addressing them advice and admonition which they do not understand.[2] The more intelligent and enterprising among the

[1] Cf. *Voraussetzungen des Sozialismus*, especially the first two (critical) chapters. Bernstein's reverent attitude toward Marx and Engels, as well as his somewhat old-fashioned conception of the scope and method of science, gives his discussion an air of much greater consonance with the orthodox Marxism than it really has. In his later expressions this consonance and conciliatory animus show up more strongly rather than otherwise. (See *Socialism and Science*, including the special preface written for the French edition.) That which was to Marx and Engels the point of departure and the guiding norm—the Hegelian dialectic—is to Bernstein a mistake from which scientific socialism must free itself. He says, *e.g.*, (*Voraussetzungen*, end of ch. iv.), "The great things achieved by Marx and Engels they have achieved not by the help of the Hegelian dialectic, but in spite of it."

The number of the "revisionists" is very considerable, and they are plainly gaining ground as against the Marxists of the older line of orthodoxy. They are by no means agreed among themselves as to details, but they belong together by virtue of their endeavor to so construe (and amend) the Marxian system as to bring it into consonance with the current scientific point of view. One should rather say points of view, since the revisionist endeavors are not all directed to bringing the received views in under a single point of view. There are two main directions of movement among the revisionists: (*a*) those who, like Bernstein, Conrad Schmidt, Tugan-Baranowski, Labriola, Ferri, aim to bring Marxism abreast of the standpoint of modern science, essentially Darwinists; and (*b*) those who aim to return to some footing on the level of the romantic philosophy. The best type and the strongest of the latter class are the neo-Kantians, embodying that spirit of revulsion to romantic norms of theory that makes up the philosophical side of the reactionary movement fostered by the discipline of German imperialism. (See K. Vorländer, *Die neukantische Bewegung im Sozialismus*.)

Except that he is not officially inscribed in the socialist calendar, Sombart might be cited as a particularly effective revisionist, so far as concerns the point of modernizing Marxism and putting the modernized materialistic conception to work.

[2] *Cf.* the files of the *Neue Zeit*, particularly during the controversy with Bernstein, and *Bernstein und das Sozialdemokratische Programm*.

idealist wing—where intellectual enterprise is not a particularly obvious trait—have been struggling to speak for the view that the forces of the environment may effectually reach men's spiritual life thru other avenues than the calculus of the main chance, and so may give rise to habitual ideals and aspirations independent of, and possibly alien to, that calculus.[1]

So, again, as to the doctrine of the class struggle. In the Marxian scheme of dialectical evolution the development which is in this way held to be controlled by the material exigencies must, it is held, proceed by the method of the class struggle. This class struggle is held to be inevitable, and is held inevitably to lead at each revolutionary epoch to a more efficient adjustment of human industry to human uses, because, when a large proportion of the community find themselves ill served by the current economic arrangements, they take thought, band together, and enforce a readjustment more equitable and more advantageous to them. So long as differences of economic advantage prevail, there will be a divergence of interests between those more advantageously placed and those less advantageously placed. The members of society will take sides as this line of cleavage indicated by their several economic interests may decide. Class solidarity will arise on the basis of this class interest, and a struggle between the two classes so marked off against each other will set in,—a struggle which, in the logic of the situation, can end only when the previously less fortunate class gains the ascendency,—and so must the class struggle proceed until it shall have

---

[1] The "idealist" socialists are even more in evidence outside of Germany. They may fairly be said to be in the ascendant in France, and they are a very strong and free-spoken contingent of the socialist movement of America. They do not commonly speak the language either of science or of philosophy, but, so far as their contentions may be construed from the standpoint of modern science, their drift seems to be something of the kind indicated above. At the same time the spokesmen of this scattering and shifting group stand for a variety of opinions and aspirations that cannot be classified under Marxism, Darwinism, or any other system of theory. At the margin they shade off into theology and the creeds.

put an end to that diversity of economic interest on which the class struggle rests. All this is logically consistent and convincing, but it proceeds on the ground of reasoned conduct, calculus of advantage, not on the ground of cause and effect. The class struggle so conceived should always and everywhere tend unremittingly toward the socialistic consummation, and should reach that consummation in the end, whatever obstructions or diversions might retard the sequence of development along the way. Such is the notion of it embodied in the system of Marx. Such, however, is not the showing of history. Not all nations or civilizations have advanced unremittingly toward a socialistic consummation, in which all divergence of economic interest has lapsed or would lapse. Those nations and civilizations which have decayed and failed, as nearly all known nations and civilizations have done, illustrate the point that, however reasonable and logical the advance by means of the class struggle may be, it is by no means inevitable. Under the Darwinian norm it must be held that men's reasoning is largely controlled by other than logical, intellectual forces; that the conclusion reached by public or class opinion is as much, or more, a matter of sentiment than of logical inference; and that the sentiment which animates men, singly or collectively, is as much, or more, an outcome of habit and native propensity as of calculated material interest. There is, for instance, no warrant in the Darwinian scheme of things for asserting *a priori* that the class interest of the working class will bring them to take a stand against the propertied class. It may as well be that their training in subservience to their employers will bring them again to realize the equity and excellence of the established system of subjection and unequal distribution of wealth. Again, no one, for instance, can tell to-day what will be the outcome of the present situation in Europe and America. It may be that the working classes will go forward along the line of the socialistic ideals and enforce a new deal, in which there shall be no economic class discrepancies, no international animosity, no dynastic politics. But then it may also, so far as can be foreseen, equally well happen that the working class, with the rest of the community in Germany, England, or America, will be led by the habit of loyalty and by their sportsmanlike propensities to lend themselves enthusiastically to the game of dynastic politics which alone their sportsmanlike rulers consider worth while. It is quite impossible on Darwinian ground to foretell whether the "proletariat" will go on to establish the socialistic revolution or turn aside again, and sink their force in the broad sands of patriotism. It is a question of habit and native propensity and of the range of stimuli to which the proletariat are exposed and are to be exposed, and what may be the outcome is not a matter of logical consistency, but of response to stimulus.

So, then, since Darwinian concepts have begun to dominate the thinking of the Marxists, doubts have now and again come to assert themselves both as to the inevitableness of the irrepressible class struggle and to its sole efficacy. Anything like a violent class struggle, a seizure of power by force, is more and more consistently deprecated. For resort to force, it is felt, brings in its train coercive control with all its apparatus of prerogative, mastery, and subservience.[1]

So, again, the Marxian doctrine of progressive proletarian distress, the so-called *Verelendungstheorie*, which stands pat on the romantic ground of the original Marxism, has fallen into abeyance, if not into disrepute, since the Darwinian conceptions have come to prevail. As a matter of reasoned procedure, on the ground of enlightened material interest alone, it should be a tenable position that increasing misery, increasing in degree and in volume, should be the outcome of the present system of ownership, and should at the same time result in a well-advised and

---

[1] Thruout the revisionist literature in Germany there is visible a softening of the traits of the doctrine of the class struggle, and the like shows itself in the programs of the party. Outside of Germany the doctrinaire insistence on this tenet is weakening even more decidedly. The opportunist politicians, with strong aspirations, but with relatively few and ill-defined theoretical preconceptions, are gaining ground.

well-consolidated working-class movement that would replace the present system by a scheme more advantageous to the majority. But so soon as the question is approached on the Darwinian ground of cause and effect, and is analyzed in terms of habit and of response to stimulus, the doctrine that progressive misery must effect a socialistic revolution becomes dubious, and very shortly untenable. Experience, the experience of history, teaches that abject misery carries with it deterioration and abject subjection. The theory of progressive distress fits convincingly into the scheme of the Hegelian three-phase dialectic. It stands for the antithesis that is to be merged in the ulterior synthesis; but it has no particular force on the ground of an argument from cause to effect.[1]

It fares not much better with the Marxian theory of value and its corollaries and dependent doctrines when Darwinian concepts are brought in to replace the romantic elements out of which it is built up. Its foundation is the metaphysical equality between the volume of human life force productively spent in the making of goods and the magnitude of these goods considered as human products. The question of such an equality has no meaning in terms of cause and effect, nor does it bear in any intelligible way upon the Darwinian question of the fitness of any given system of production or distribution. In any evolutionary system of economics the central question touching the efficiency and fitness of any given system of production is necessarily the question as to the excess of serviceability in the product over the cost of production.[2] It is in such an excess of serviceability over cost

---

[1] *Cf.* Bernstein, *Die heutige Sozialdemokratie in Theorie und Praxis*, an answer to Brunhuber, *Die heutige Sozialdemokratie*, which should be consulted in the same connection; Goldscheid, *Verelendungs- oder Meliorationstheorie*; also Sombart, *Sozialismus und soziale Bewegung*, 5th edition, pp. 86-89.

[2] Accordingly, in later Marxian handling of the questions of exploitation and accumulation, the attention is centred on the "surplus product" rather than on the "surplus value." It is also currently held that the doctrines and practical consequences which Marx derived from the theory of surplus

that the chance of survival lies for any system of production, in so far as the question of survival is a question of production, and this matter comes into the speculation of Marx only indirectly or incidentally, and leads to nothing in his argument.

And, as bearing on the Marxian doctrines of exploitation, there is on Darwinian ground no place for a natural right to the full product of labor. What can be argued in that connection on the ground of cause and effect simply is the question as to what scheme of distribution will help or hinder the survival of a given people or a given civilization.[1]

But these questions of abstruse theory need not be pursued, since they count, after all, but relatively little among the working tenets of the movement. Little need be done by the Marxists to work out or to adapt the Marxian system of value theory, since it has but slight bearing on the main question,—the question of the trend towards socialism and of its chances of success. It is conceivable that a competent theory of value dealing with the excess of serviceability over cost, on the one hand, and with the discrepancy between price and serviceability, on the other hand, would have a substantial bearing upon the advisability of the present as against the socialistic régime, and would go far to clear up the notions of both socialists and conservatives as to the nature of the points in dispute between them. But the socialists

---

value would remain substantially well founded, even if the theory of surplus value were given up. These secondary doctrines could be saved—at the cost of orthodoxy—by putting a theory of surplus product in the place of the theory of surplus value, as in effect is done by Bernstein (*Sozialdemokratie in Theorie und Praxis*, sec. 5. Also various of the essays included in *Zur Geschichte und Theorie des Sozialismus*).

[1] The "right to the full product of labor" and the Marxian theory of exploitation associated with that principle has fallen into the background, except as a campaign cry designed to stir the emotions of the working class. Even as a campaign cry it has not the prominence, nor apparently the efficacy, which it once had. The tenet is better preserved, in fact, among the "idealists," who draw for their antecedents on the French Revolution and the English philosophy of natural rights, than among the latter-day Marxists.

have not moved in the direction of this problem, and they have the excuse that their critics have suggested neither a question nor a solution to a question along any such line. None of the value theorists have so far offered anything that could be called good, bad, or indifferent in this connection, and the socialists are as innocent as the rest. Economics, indeed, has not at this point yet begun to take on a modern tone, unless the current neglect of value theory by the socialists be taken as a negative symptom of advance, indicating that they at least recognize the futility of the received problems and solutions, even if they are not ready to make a positive move.

• • •

The shifting of the current point of view, from romantic philosophy to matter-of-fact, has affected the attitude of the Marxists towards the several articles of theory more than it has induced an avowed alteration or a substitution of new elements of theory for the old. It is always possible to make one's peace with a new standpoint by new interpretations and a shrewd use of figures of speech, so far as the theoretical formulation is concerned, and something of this kind has taken place in the case of Marxism; but when, as in the case of Marxism, the formulations of theory are drafted into practical use, substantial changes of appreciable magnitude are apt to show themselves in a changed attitude towards practical questions. The Marxists have had to face certain practical problems, especially problems of party tactics, and the substantial changes wrought in their theoretical outlook have come into evidence here. The real gravity of the changes that have overtaken Marxism would scarcely be seen by a scrutiny of the formal professions of the Marxists alone. But the exigencies of a changing situation have provoked readjustments of the received doctrinal position, and the shifting of the philosophical standpoint and postulates has come into evidence as marking the limits of change in their professions which the socialistic doctrinaires could allow themselves.

The changes comprised in the cultural movement that lies between the middle and the close of the nineteenth century are great and grave, at least as seen from so near a standpoint as the present day, and it is safe to say that, in whatever historical perspective they may be seen, they must, in some respects, always assert themselves as unprecedented. So far as concerns the present topic, there are three main lines of change that have converged upon the Marxist system of doctrines, and have led to its latter-day modification and growth. One of these—the change in the postulates of knowledge, in the metaphysical foundations of theory—has been spoken of already, and its bearing on the growth of socialist theory has been indicated in certain of its general features. But, among the circumstances that have conditioned the growth of the system, the most obvious is the fact that since Marx's time his doctrines have come to serve as the platform of a political movement, and so have been exposed to the stress of practical party politics dealing with a new and changing situation. At the same time the industrial (economic) situation to which the doctrines are held to apply—of which they are the theoretical formulation—has also in important respects changed its character from what it was when Marx first formulated his views. These several lines of cultural change affecting the growth of Marxism cannot be held apart in so distinct a manner as to appraise the work of each separately. They belong inextricably together, as do the effects wrought by them in the system.

In practical politics the Social Democrats have had to make up their account with the labor movement, the agricultural population, and the imperialistic policy. On each of these heads the preconceived program of Marxism has come in conflict with the run of events, and on each head it has been necessary to deal shrewdly and adapt the principles to the facts of the time. The adaptation to circumstances has not been altogether of the nature of compromise, altho here and there the spirit of compromise and conciliation is visible enough. A conciliatory party policy may, of course, impose an adaptation of form and color upon the party principles, without thereby seriously affecting the substance of the principles themselves; but the need of a conciliatory policy may, even more, provoke a substantial change of attitude toward practical questions in a case where a shifting of the theoretical point of view makes room for a substantial change.

Apart from all merely tactical expedients, the experience of the past thirty years has led the German Marxists to see the facts of the labor situation in a new light, and has induced them to attach an altered meaning to the accepted formulations of doctrine. The facts have not freely lent themselves to the scheme of the Marxist system, but the scheme has taken on such a new meaning as would be consistent with the facts. The untroubled Marxian economics, such as it finds expression in the *Kapital* and earlier documents of the theory, has no place and no use for a trade-union movement, or, indeed, for any similar non-political organization among the working class, and the attitude of the Social-Democratic leaders of opinion in the early days of the party's history was accordingly hostile to any such movement,[1]—as much so, indeed, as the loyal adherents of the classical political economy. That was before the modern industrial era had got under way in Germany, and therefore before the German socialistic doctrinaires had learned by experience what the development of industry was to bring with it. It was also before the modern scientific postulates had begun to disintegrate the neo-Hegelian preconceptions as to the logical sequence in the development of institutions.

[1] It is, of course, well known that even in the transactions and pronunciamentos of the International a good word is repeatedly said for the trade-unions and both the Gotha and the Erfurt programs speak in favor of labor organizations, and put forth demands designed to further the trade-union endeavors. But it is equally well known that these expressions were in good part perfunctory, and that the substantial motive behind them was the politic wish of the socialists to conciliate the unionists, and make use of the unions for the propaganda. The early expressions of sympathy with the unionist cause were made for an ulterior purpose. Later on, in the nineties, there comes a change in the attitude of the socialist leaders toward the unions.

In Germany, as elsewhere, the growth of the capitalistic system presently brought on trade-unionism; that is to say, it brought on an organized attempt on the part of the workmen to deal with the questions of capitalistic production and distribution by business methods, to settle the problems of working-class employment and livelihood by a system of non-political, businesslike bargains. But the great point of all socialist aspiration and endeavor is the abolition of all business and all bargaining, and, accordingly, the Social Democrats were heartily out of sympathy with the unions and their endeavors to make business terms with the capitalist system, and make life tolerable for the workmen under that system. But the union movement grew to be so serious a feature of the situation that the socialists found themselves obliged to deal with unions, since they could not deal with the workmen over the heads of the unions. The Social Democrats, and therefore the Marxian theorists, had to deal with a situation which included the union movement, and this movement was bent on improving the workman's conditions of life from day to day. Therefore it was necessary to figure out how the union movement could and must further the socialistic advance; to work into the body of doctrines a theory of how the unions belong in the course of economic development that leads up to socialism, and to reconcile the unionist efforts at improvement with the ends of Social Democracy. Not only were the unions seeking improvement by unsocialistic methods, but the level of comfort among the working classes was in some respects advancing, apparently as a result of these union efforts. Both the huckstering animus of the workmen in their unionist policy and the possible amelioration of working-class conditions had to be incorporated into the socialistic platform and into the Marxist theory of economic development. The Marxist theory of progressive misery and degradation has, accordingly, fallen into the background, and a large proportion of the Marxists have already come to see the whole question of working-class deterioration in some such apologetic light as is shed upon it by Goldscheid in his *Verelendungs-oder Meliorationstheorie*. It is now not an unusual thing for orthodox Marxists to hold that the improvement of the conditions of the working classes is a necessary condition to the advance of the socialistic cause, and that the unionist efforts at amelioration must be furthered as a means toward the socialistic consummation. It is recognized that the socialistic revolution must be carried through not by an anæmic working class under the pressure of abject privation, but by a body of full-blooded workingmen gradually gaining strength from improved conditions of life. Instead of the revolution being worked out by the leverage of desperate misery, every improvement in working-class conditions is to be counted as a gain for the revolutionary forces. This is a good Darwinism, but it does not belong in the neo-Hegelian Marxism.

Perhaps the sorest experience of the Marxist doctrinaires has been with the agricultural population. Notoriously, the people of the open country have not taken kindly to socialism. No propaganda and no changes in the economic situation have won the sympathy of the peasant farmers for the socialistic revolution. Notoriously, too, the large-scale industry has not invaded the agricultural field, or expropriated the small proprietors, in anything like the degree expected by the Marxist doctrinaires of a generation ago. It is contained in the theoretical system of Marx that, as modern industrial and business methods gain ground, the small proprietor farmers will be reduced to the ranks of the wage-proletariat, and that, as this process of conversion goes on, in the course of time the class interest of the agricultural population will throw them into the movement side by side with the other wage-workmen.[1] But at this point the facts have hitherto not come out in consonance with the Marxist theory. And the efforts of the Social Democrats to convert the peasant population to socialism have been practically unrewarded. So it has come about that the political leaders and the keepers of the doctrines have, tardily and reluctantly, come to see the facts of

---

[1] Cf. *Capital*, vol. i., ch. xiii., sect. 10.

the agrarian situation in a new light, and to give a new phrasing to the articles of Marxian theory that touch on the fortunes of the peasant farmer. It is no longer held that either the small properties of the peasant farmer must be absorbed into larger properties, and then taken over by the State, or that they must be taken over by the State directly, when the socialistic revolution is established. On the contrary, it is now coming to be held that the peasant proprietors will not be disturbed in their holdings by the great change. The great change is to deal with capitalistic enterprise, and the peasant farming is not properly "capitalistic." It is a system of production in which the producer normally gets only the product of his own labor. Indeed, under the current régime of markets and credit relations, the small agricultural producer, it is held, gets less than the product of his own labor, since the capitalistic business enterprises with which he has to deal are always able to take advantage of him. So it has become part of the overt doctrine of socialists that as regards the peasant farmer it will be the consistent aim of the movement to secure him in the untroubled enjoyment of his holding, and free him from the vexatious exactions of his creditors and the ruinous business traffic in which he is now perforce involved. According to the revised code, made possible by recourse to Darwinian concepts of evolution instead of the Hegelian three-phase dialectic, therefore, and contrary to the earlier prognostications of Marx, it is no longer held that agricultural industry must go thru the capitalistic mill, and it is hoped that under the revised code it may be possible to enlist the interest and sympathy of this obstinately conservative element for the revolutionary cause. The change in the official socialist position on the agricultural question has come about only lately, and is scarcely yet complete, and there is no knowing what degree of success it may meet with either as a matter of party tactics or as a feature of the socialistic theory of economic development. All discussions of party policy, and of theory so far as bears on policy, take up the question; and nearly all authoritative spokesmen of socialism have modified their views in the course of time on this point.

The socialism of Karl Marx is characteristically inclined to peaceable measures and disinclined to a coercive government and belligerent politics. It is, or at least it was, strongly averse to international jealousy and patriotic animosity, and has taken a stand against armaments, wars, and dynastic aggrandizement. At the time of the French-Prussian war the official organization of Marxism, the International, went so far in its advocacy of peace as to urge the soldiery on both sides to refuse to fight. After the campaign had warmed the blood of the two nations, this advocacy of peace made the International odious in the eyes of both French and Germans. War begets patriotism, and the socialists fell under the reproach of not being sufficiently patriotic. After the conclusion of the war the Socialistic Workingmen's Party of Germany sinned against the German patriotic sentiment in a similar way and with similarly grave results. Since the foundation of the empire and of the Social-Democratic party, the socialists and their doctrines have passed thru a further experience of a similar kind, but on a larger scale and more protracted. The government has gradually strengthened its autocratic position at home, increased its warlike equipment, and enlarged its pretensions in international politics, until what would have seemed absurdly impossible a generation ago is now submitted to by the German people, not only with a good grace, but with enthusiasm. During all this time that part of the population that has adhered to the socialist ideals has also grown gradually more patriotic and more loyal, and the leaders and keepers of socialist opinion have shared in the growth of chauvinism with the rest of the German people. But at no time have the socialists been able to keep abreast of the general upward movement in this respect. They have not attained the pitch of reckless loyalty that animates the conservative German patriots, although it is probably safe to say that the Social Democrats of to-day are as good and headlong patriots as the conservative Germans were a generation ago. During all this period of the new era of German political life the socialists have been freely accused of disloyalty to the national ambition, of placing their international aspirations above the ambition of imperial aggrandizement.

The socialist spokesmen have been continually on the defensive. They set out with a round opposition to any considerable military establishment, and have more and more apologetically continued to oppose any "undue" extension of the warlike establishments and the warlike policy. But with the passage of time and the habituation to warlike politics and military discipline, the infection of jingoism has gradually permeated the body of Social Democrats, until they have now reached such a pitch of enthusiastic loyalty as they would not patiently hear a truthful characterization of. The spokesmen now are concerned to show that, while they still stand for international socialism, consonant with their ancient position, they stand for national aggrandizement first and for international comity second. The relative importance of the national and the international ideals in German socialist professions has been reversed since the seventies.[1] The leaders are busy with interpretation of their earlier formulations. They have come to excite themselves over nebulous distinctions between patriotism and jingoism. The Social Democrats have come to be German patriots first and socialists second, which comes to saying that they are a political party working for the maintenance of the existing order, with modifications. They are no longer a party of revolution, but of reform, tho the measure of reform which they demand greatly exceeds the Hohenzollern limit of tolerance. They are now as much, if not more, in touch with the ideas of English liberalism than with those of revolutionary Marxism.

The material and tactical exigencies that have grown out of changes in the industrial system and in the political situation, then, have brought on far-reaching changes of adaptation in the position of the socialists. The change may not be extremely

---

1 *Cf.* Kautsky, *Erfurter Programm*, ch. v., sect. 13; Bernstein, *Voraussetzungen*, ch. iv., sect. e.

large at any one point, so far as regards the specific articles of the program, but, taken as a whole, the resulting modification of the socialistic position is a very substantial one. The process of change is, of course, not yet completed,—whether or not it ever will be,—but it is already evident that what is taking place is not so much a change in amount or degree of conviction on certain given points as a change in kind,—a change in the current socialistic habit of mind.

The factional discrepancies of theory that have occupied the socialists of Germany for some years past are evidence that the conclusion, even a provisional conclusion, of the shifting of their standpoint has not been reached. It is even hazardous to guess which way the drift is setting. It is only evident that the past standpoint, the standpoint of neo-Hegelian Marxism, cannot be regained,—it is a forgotten standpoint. For the immediate present the drift of sentiment, at least among the educated, seems to set toward a position resembling that of the National Socials and the Rev. Mr. Naumann; that is to say, imperialistic liberalism. Should the conditions, political, social, and economic, which to-day are chiefly effective in shaping the habits of thought among the German people, continue substantially unchanged and continue to be the chief determining causes, it need surprise no one to find German socialism gradually changing into a somewhat characterless imperialistic democracy. The imperial policy seems in a fair way to get the better of revolutionary socialism, not by repressing it, but by force of the discipline in imperialistic ways of thinking to which it subjects all classes of the population. How far a similar process of sterilization is under way, or is likely to overtake the socialist movement in other countries, is an obscure question to which the German object-lesson affords no certain answer.

Thorstein Veblen.

Stanford University.

Some Neglected Points in the Theory of Socialism

Some Neglected Points in the Theory of Socialism[1]

The immediate occasion for the writing of this paper was by the publication of Mr. Spencer's essay, "From Freedom to Bondage";[2] although it is not altogether a criticism of that essay. It is not my purpose to controvert the position taken by Mr. Spencer as regards the present feasibility of any socialist scheme. The paper is mainly a suggestion, offered in the spirit of the disciple, with respect to a point not adequately covered by Mr. Spencer's discussion, and which has received but very scanty attention at the hands of any other writer on either side of the socialist controversy. This main point is as to an economic ground, as a matter of fact, for the existing unrest that finds expression in the demands of socialist agitators.

I quote from Mr. Spencer's essay a sentence which does fair justice, so far as it goes, to the position taken by agitators: "In presence of obvious improvements, joined with that increase of longevity, which even alone yields conclusive proof of general amelioration, it is proclaimed, with increasing vehemence, that things are so bad that society must be pulled to pieces and

---

[1] Published in *The Annals of the American Academy of Political and Social Science*, Vol. 2 (Nov., 1891), pp. 57-74.
[2] Introductory paper of "A Plea for Liberty"; edited by Thomas Mackay.

reorganized on another plan." The most obtrusive feature of the change demanded by the advocates of socialism is governmental control of the industrial activities of society—the nationalization of industry. There is also, just at present, a distinct movement in practice, towards a more extended control of industry by the government, as Mr. Spencer has pointed out. This movement strengthens the position of the advocates of a complete national-ization of industry, by making it appear that the logic of events is on their side.

In America at least, this movement in the direction of a broader assertion of the paramount claims of the community, and an extension of corporate action on part of the community in industrial matters, has not generally been connected with or based on an adherence to socialistic dogmas. This is perhaps truer of the recent past than of the immediate present. The motive of the movement has been, in large part, the expediency of each particular step taken. Municipal supervision, and, possibly, com-plete municipal control, has come to be a necessity in the case of such industries—mostly of recent growth—as elementary edu-cation, street-lighting, water-supply, etc. Opinions differ widely as to how far the community should take into its own hands such industries as concern the common welfare, but the growth of sentiment may fairly be said to favor a wider scope of govern-mental control.

But the necessity of some supervision in the interest of the public extends to industries which are not simply of municipal importance. The modern development of industry and of the industrial organization of society makes it increasingly necessary that certain industries—often spoken of as "natural monopo-lies"—should be treated as being of a semi-public character. And through the action of the same forces a constantly increasing number of occupations are developing into the form of "natural monopolies."

The motive of the movement towards corporate action on the part of the community—State control of industry—has been largely that of industrial expediency. But another motive has gone with this one, and has grown more prominent as the popular demands in this direction have gathered wider support and taken more definite form. The injustice, the inequality, of the existing system, so far as concerns these natural monopolies especially, are made much of. There is a distinct unrest abroad, a discontent with things as they are, and the cry of injustice is the expression of this more or less widely prevalent discontent. This discontent is the truly socialistic element in the situation.

It is easy to make too much of this popular unrest. The clamor of the agitators might be taken to indicate a wider prevalence and a greater acuteness of popular discontent than actually exists; but after all due allowance is made for exaggeration on the part of those interested in the agitation, there can still be no doubt of the presence of a chronic feeling of dissatisfaction with the working of the existing industrial system, and a growth of popular sentiment in favor of a leveling policy. The economic ground of this popular feeling must be found, if we wish to understand the significance, for our industrial system, of the movement to which it supplies the motive. If its causes shall appear to be of a transient character, there is little reason to apprehend a permanent or radical change of our industrial system as the outcome of the agitation; while if this popular sentiment is found to be the outgrowth of any of the essential features of the existing social system, the chances of its ultimately working a radical change in the system will be much greater.

The explanation offered by Mr. Spencer, that the popular unrest is due essentially to a feeling of *ennui*—to a desire for a change of posture on part of the social body, is assuredly not to be summarily rejected; but the analogy will hardly serve to explain the sentiment away. This may be a cause, but it can hardly be accepted as a sufficient cause.

Socialist agitators urge that the existing system is necessarily wasteful and industrially inefficient. That may be granted, but it does not serve to explain the popular discontent, because the popular opinion, in which the discontent resides, does notoriously not favor that view. They further urge that the existing system is unjust, in that it gives an advantage to one man over another. That contention may also be true, but it is in itself no explanation, for it is true only if it be granted that the institutions which make this advantage of one man over another possible are unjust, and that is begging the question. This last contention is, however, not so far out of line with popular sentiment. The advantage complained of lies, under modern conditions, in the possession of property, and there is a feeling abroad that the existing order of things affords an undue advantage to property, especially to owners of property whose possessions rise much above a certain rather indefinite average. This feeling of injured justice is not always distinguishable from envy; but it is, at any rate, a factor that works towards a leveling policy. With it goes a feeling of slighted manhood, which works in the same direction. Both these elements are to a great extent of a subjective origin. They express themselves in the general, objective form, but it is safe to say that on the average they spring from a consciousness of disadvantage and slight suffered by the person expressing them, and by persons whom he classes with himself. No flippancy is intended in saying that the rich are not so generally alive to the necessity of any leveling policy as are people of slender means. Any question as to the legitimacy of the dissatisfaction, on moral grounds, or even on grounds of expediency, is not very much to the point; the question is as to its scope and its chances of persistence.

The modern industrial system is based on the institution of private property under free competition, and it cannot be claimed that these institutions have heretofore worked to the detriment of the material interests of the average member of society. The ground of discontent cannot lie in a disadvantageous comparison of the present with the past, so far as material interests are concerned. It is notorious, and, practically, none of the agitators deny, that the system of industrial competition, based on private property, has brought about, or has at least co-existed with, the most rapid advance in average wealth and industrial efficiency that the world has seen. Especially can it fairly be claimed that the result of the last few decades of our industrial development has been to increase greatly the creature comforts within the reach of the average human being. And, decidedly, the result has been an amelioration of the lot of the less favored in a relatively greater degree than that of those economically more fortunate. The claim that the system of competition has proved itself an engine for making the rich richer and the poor poorer has the fascination of epigram; but if its meaning is that the lot of the average, of the masses of humanity in civilized life, is worse to-day, as measured in the means of livelihood, than it was twenty, or fifty, or a hundred years ago, then it is farcical. The cause of discontent must be sought elsewhere than in any increased difficulty in obtaining the means of subsistence or of comfort. But there is a sense in which the aphorism is true, and in it lies at least a partial explanation of the unrest which our conservative people so greatly deprecate. The existing system has not made, and does not tend to make, the industrious poor poorer as measured absolutely in means of livelihood; but it does tend to make them relatively poorer, in their own eyes, as measured in terms of comparative economic importance, and, curious as it may seem at first sight, that is what seems to count. It is not the abjectly poor that are oftenest heard protesting; and when a protest is heard in their behalf it is through spokesmen who are from outside their own class, and who are not delegated to speak for them. They are not a negligible element in the situation, but the unrest which is ground for solicitude does not owe its importance to them. The protest comes from those who do not habitually, or of necessity, suffer physical privation. The qualification "of necessity," is to be noticed. There is a not inconsiderable amount of physical privation suffered by many people in this country, which is not physically necessary. The cause is very often that what might be the means of comfort is diverted to the purpose of maintaining a decent appearance, or even a show of luxury.

Man as we find him to-day has much regard to his good

fame—to his standing in the esteem of his fellow-men. This characteristic he always has had, and no doubt always will have. This regard for reputation may take the noble form of a striving after a good name; but the existing organization of society does not in any way pre-eminently foster that line of development. Regard for one's reputation means, in the average of cases, emulation. It is a striving to be, and more immediately to be thought to be, better than one's neighbor. Now, modern society, the society in which competition without prescription is predominant, is pre-eminently an industrial, economic society, and it is industrial—economic—excellence that most readily attracts the approving regard of that society. Integrity and personal worth will, of course, count for something, now as always; but in the case of a person of moderate pretentions and opportunities, such as the average of us are, one's reputation for excellence in this direction does not penetrate far enough into the very wide environment to which a person is exposed in modern society to satisfy even a very modest craving for respectability. To sustain one's dignity—and to sustain one's self-respect—under the eyes of people who are not socially one's immediate neighbors, it is necessary to display the token of economic worth, which practically coincides pretty closely with economic success. A person may be well-born and virtuous, but those attributes will not bring respect to the bearer from people who are not aware of his possessing them, and these are ninety-nine out of every one hundred that one meets. Conversely, by the way, knavery and vulgarity in any person are not reprobated by people who know nothing of the person's shortcomings in those respects.

In our fundamentally industrial society a person should be economically successful, if he would enjoy the esteem of his fellowmen. When we say that a man is "worth" so many dollars, the expression does not convey the idea that moral or other personal excellence is to be measured in terms of money, but it does very distinctly convey the idea that the fact of his possessing many dollars is very much to his credit. And, except in cases of extraordinary excellence, efficiency in any direction which is not immediately of industrial importance, and does not redound to a person's economic benefit, is not of great value as a means of respectability. Economic success is in our day the most widely accepted as well as the most readily ascertainable measure of esteem. All this will hold with still greater force of a generation which is born into a world already encrusted with this habit of a mind.

But there is a further, secondary stage in the development of this economic emulation. It is not enough to possess the talisman of industrial success. In order that it may mend one's good fame efficiently, it is necessary to display it. One does not "make much of a showing" in the eyes of the large majority of the people whom one meets with, except by unremitting demonstration of ability to pay. That is practically the only means which the average of us have of impressing our respectability on the many to whom we are personally unknown, but whose transient good opinion we would so gladly enjoy. So it comes about that the appearance of success is very much to be desired, and is even in many cases preferred to the substance. We all know how nearly indispensable it is to afford whatever expenditure other people with whom we class ourselves can afford, and also that it is desirable to afford a little something more than others.

This element of human nature has much to do with the "standard of living." And it is of a very elastic nature, capable of an indefinite extension. After making proper allowance for individual exceptions and for the action of prudential restraints, it may be said, in a general way, that this emulation in expenditure stands ever ready to absorb any margin of income that remains after ordinary physical wants and comforts have been provided for, and, further, that it presently becomes as hard to give up that part of one's habitual "standard of living" which is due to the struggle for respectability, as it is to give up many physical comforts. In a general way, the need of expenditure in this direction grows as fast as the means of satisfying it, and, in the long run, a large expenditure comes no nearer satisfying the desire than a smaller one.

It comes about through the working of this principle that even the creature comforts, which are in themselves desirable, and, it may even be, requisite to a life on a passably satisfactory plane, acquire a value as a means of respectability quite independent of, and out of proportion to, their simple utility as a means of livelihood. As we are all aware, the chief element of value in many articles of apparel is not their efficiency for protecting the body, but for protecting the wearer's respectability; and that not only in the eyes of one's neighbors but even in one's own eyes. Indeed, it happens not very rarely that a person chooses to go ill-clad in order to be well dressed. Much more than half the value of what is worn by the American people may confidently be put down to the element of "dress," rather than to that of "clothing." And the chief motive of dress is emulation—what I have ventured to designate as "economic emulation." The like is true, though perhaps in a less degree, of what goes to food and shelter.

This misdirection of effort through the cravings of human vanity is of course not anything new, nor is "economic emulation" a modern fact. The modern system of industry has not invented emulation, nor has even this particular form of emulation originated under that system. But the system of free competition has accentuated this form of emulation, both by exalting the industrial activity of man above the rank which it held under more primitive forms of social organization, and by in great measure cutting off other forms of emulation from the chance of efficiently ministering to the craving for a good fame. Speaking generally and from the standpoint of the average man, the modern industrial organization of society has practically narrowed the scope of emulation to this one line; and at the same time it has made the means of sustenance and comfort so much easier to obtain as very materially to widen the margin of human exertion that can be devoted to purposes of emulation. Further, by increasing the freedom of movement of the individual and widening the environment to which the individual is exposed—increasing the number of persons before whose eyes each one carries on his life, and, *pari passu*, decreasing the chances which such persons have of awarding their esteem on any other basis than that of immediate appearances, it has increased the relative efficiency of the economic means of winning respect through a show of expenditure for personal comforts.

It is not probable that further advance in the same direction will lead to a different result in the immediate future; and it is the *immediate* future we have to deal with. A further advance in the efficiency of our industry, and a further widening of the human environment to which the individual is exposed, should logically render emulation in this direction more intense. There are, indeed, certain considerations to be set off against this tendency, but they are mostly factors of slow action, and are hardly of sufficient consequence to reverse the general rule. On the whole, other things remaining the same, it must be admitted that, within wide limits, the easier the conditions of physical life for modern civilized man become, and the wider the horizon of each and the extent of the personal contact of each with his fellowmen, and the greater the opportunity of each to compare notes with his fellows, the greater will be the preponderance of economic success as a means of emulation, and the greater the straining after economic respectability. Inasmuch as the aim of emulation is not any absolute degree of comfort or of excellence, no advance in the average well-being of the community can end the struggle or lessen the strain. A general amelioration cannot quiet the unrest whose source is the craving of everybody to compare favorably with his neighbor.

Human nature being what it is, the struggle of each to possess more than his neighbor is inseparable from the institution of private property. And also, human nature being what it is, one who possesses less will, on the average, be jealous of the one who possesses more; and "more" means not more than the average share, but more than the share of the person who makes the comparison. The criterion of complacency is, largely, the *de facto* possession or enjoyment; and the present growth of sentiment among the body of the people—who possess less—favors, in a vague way, a readjustment adverse to the interests of those who possess more, and adverse to the possibility of legitimately possessing or enjoying "more;" that is to say, the growth of sentiment favors a socialistic movement. The outcome of modern industrial development has been, so far as concerns the present purpose, to intensify emulation and the jealousy that goes with emulation, and to focus the emulation and the jealousy on the possession and enjoyment of material goods. The ground of the unrest with which we are concerned is, very largely, jealousy,—envy, if you choose; and the ground of this particular form of jealousy, that makes for socialism, is to be found in the institution of private property. With private property, under modern conditions, this jealousy and unrest are unavoidable.

The corner-stone of the modern industrial system is the institution of private property. That institution is also the objective point of all attacks upon the existing system of competitive industry, whether open or covert, whether directed against the system as a whole or against any special feature of it. It is, moreover, the ultimate ground—and, under modern conditions, necessarily so—of the unrest and discontent whose proximate cause is the struggle for economic respectability. The inference seems to be that, human nature being what it is, there can be no peace from this—it must be admitted—ignoble form of emulation, or from the discontent that goes with it, this side of the abolition of private property. Whether a larger measure of peace is in store for us after that event shall have come to pass, is of course not a matter to be counted on, nor is the question immediately to the point.

This economic emulation is of course not the sole motive, nor the most important feature, of modern industrial life; although it is in the foreground, and it pervades the structure of modern society more thoroughly perhaps than any other equally powerful moral factor. It would be rash to predict that socialism will be the inevitable outcome of a continued development of this emulation and the discontent which it fosters, and it is by no means the purpose of this paper to insist on such an inference. The most that can be claimed is that this emulation is one of the causes, if not the chief cause, of the existing unrest and dissatisfaction with things as they are; that this unrest is inseparable from the existing system of industrial organization; and that the growth of popular sentiment under the influence of these conditions is necessarily adverse to the institution of private property, and therefore adverse to the existing industrial system of free competition.

The emulation to which attention has been called in the preceding section of this paper is not only a fact of importance to an understanding of the unrest that is urging us towards an untried path in social development, but it has also a bearing on the question of the practicability of any scheme for the complete nationalization of industry. Modern industry has developed to such a degree of efficiency as to make the struggle for subsistence alone, under average conditions, relatively easy, as compared with the state of the case a few generations ago. As I have labored to show, the modern competitive system has at the same time given the spirit of emulation such a direction that the attainment of subsistence and comfort no longer fixes, even approximately, the limit of the required aggregate labor on the part of the community. Under modern conditions the struggle for existence has, in a very appreciable degree, been transformed into a struggle to keep up appearances. The ultimate ground of this struggle to keep up appearances by otherwise unnecessary expenditure, is the institution of private property. Under a régime which should allow no inequality of acquisition or of income, this form of emulation, which is due to the possibility of such inequality, would also tend to become obsolete. With the abolition of private property, the characteristic of human nature which now finds its exercise in this form of emulation, should logically find exercise in other, perhaps nobler and socially more serviceable, activities; it is at any rate not easy to imagine it running into any line of action more futile or less worthy of human effort.

Supposing the standard of comfort of the community to remain approximately at its present average, the abolition of the struggle to keep up economic appearances would very considerably lessen the aggregate amount of labor required for the support of the community. How great a saving of labor might be effected is not easy to say. I believe it is within the mark to suppose that the struggle to keep up appearances is chargeable, directly and indirectly, with one-half the aggregate labor, and abstinence from labor—for the standard of respectability requires us to shun labor as well as to enjoy the fruits of it—on part of the American people. This does not mean that the same community, under a system not allowing private property, could make its way with half the labor we now put forth; but it means something more or less nearly approaching that. Anyone who has not seen our modern social life from this point of view will find the claim absurdly extravagant, but the startling character of the proposition will wear off with longer and closer attention to this aspect of the facts of everyday life. But the question of the exact amount of waste due to this factor is immaterial. It will not be denied that it is a fact of considerable magnitude, and that is all that the argument requires.

It is accordingly competent for the advocates of the nationalization of industry and property to claim that even if their scheme of organization should prove less effective for production of goods than the present, as measured absolutely in terms of the aggregate output of our industry, yet the community might readily be maintained at the present average standard of comfort. The required aggregate output of the nation's industry would be considerably less than at present, and there would therefore be less necessity for that close and strenuous industrial organization and discipline of the members of society under the new régime, whose evils unfriendly critics are apt to magnify. The chances of practicability for the scheme should logically be considerably increased by this lessening of the necessity for severe application. The less irksome and exacting the new régime, the less chance of a reversion to the earlier system.

Under such a social order, where common labor would no longer be a mark of peculiar economic necessity and consequent low economic rank on part of the laborer, it is even conceivable that labor might practically come to assume that character of nobility in the eyes of society at large, which it now sometimes assumes in the speculations of the well-to-do, in their complacent moods. Much has sometimes been made of this possibility by socialist speculators, but the inference has something of a utopian look, and no one, certainly, is entitled to build institutions for the coming social order on this dubious ground.

What there seems to be ground for claiming is that a society which has reached our present degree of industrial efficiency would not go into the Socialist or Nationalist state with as many chances of failure as a community whose industrial development is still at the stage at which strenuous labor on the part of nearly all members is barely sufficient to make both ends meet.

In Mr. Spencer's essay, in conformity with the line of argument of his "Principles of Sociology," it is pointed out that, as the result of constantly operative social forces, all social systems, as regards the form of organization, fall into the one or the other of Sir Henry Maine's two classes—the system of status or the system of contract. In accordance with this generalization it is concluded that whenever the modern system of contract or free competition shall be displaced, it will necessarily be replaced by the only other known system—that of status; the type of which is the military organization, or, also, a hierarchy, or a bureaucracy. It is something after the fashion of the industrial organization of ancient Peru that Mr. Spencer pictures as the inevitable sequel of the demise of the existing competitive system. Voluntary coöperation can be replaced only by compulsory coöperation, which is identified with the system of status and defined as the subjection of man to his fellow-man.

Now, at least as a matter of speculation, this is not the only alternative. These two systems, of status, or prescription, and of contract, or competition, have divided the field of social organization between them in some proportion or other in the past. Mr. Spencer has shown that, very generally, where human progress in its advanced stages has worked towards the amelioration of the lot of the average member of society, the movement has been away from the system of status and towards the system of contract. But there is at least one, if not more than one exception to the rule, as concerns the recent past. The latest development of the industrial organization among civilized nations—perhaps in an especial degree in the case of the American people—has not been entirely a continuation of the approach to a régime of free contract. It is also, to say the least, very doubtful if the movement has been towards a régime of status, in the sense in which Sir Henry Maine uses the term. This is especially evident in the case of the great industries which we call "natural monopolies;" and it is to be added that the present tendency is for a continually increasing proportion of the industrial activities of the community to fall into the category of "natural monopolies." No revolution has been achieved; the system of competition has not been discarded, but the course of industrial development is not in the direction of an extension of that system at all points; nor does the principle of status always replace that of competition wherever the latter fails.

The classification of methods of social organization under the two heads of status or of contract, is not logically exhaustive. There is nothing in the meaning of the terms employed which will compel us to say that whenever man escapes from the control of his fellow man, under a system of status, he thereby falls into a system of free contract. There is a conceivable escape from the dilemma, and it is this conceivable, though perhaps impracticable, escape from both these systems that the socialist agitator wishes to effect. An acquaintance with the aims and position of the more advanced and consistent advocates of a new departure leaves no doubt but that the principles of contract and of status, both, are in substance familiar to their thoughts—though often in a vague and inadequate form—and that they distinctly repudiate both. This is perhaps less true of those who take the socialist position mainly on ethical grounds.

As bearing on this point it may be remarked that while the industrial system, in the case of all communities with whose history we are acquainted, has always in the past been organized according to a scheme of status or of contract, or of the two combined in some proportion, yet the social organization has not in all cases developed along the same lines, so far as concerns such social functions as are not primarily industrial. Especially is this true of the later stages in the development of those communities whose institutions we are accustomed to contemplate with the most complacency, *e.g.*, the case of the English-speaking peoples. The whole system of modern constitutional government in its latest developed forms, in theory at least, and, in a measure, in practice, does not fall under the head of either contract or status. It is the analogy of modern constitutional government through an impersonal law and impersonal institutions, that comes nearest doing justice to the vague notions of our socialist propagandists. It is true, some of the most noted among them are fond of the analogy of the military organization, as a striking illustration of one feature of the system they advocate, but that must after all be taken as an *obiter dictum*.

Further, as to the manner of the evolution of existing institutions and their relation to the two systems spoken of. So far as concerns the communities which have figured largely in the civilized world, the political organization has had its origin in a military system of government. So, also, has the industrial organization. But while the development of industry, during its gradual escape from the military system of status, has been, at least until lately, in the direction of a system of free contract, the development of the political organization, so far as it has escaped from the régime of status, has not been in that direction. The system of status is a system of subjection to personal authority,—of prescription and class distinctions, and privileges and immunities; the system of constitutional government, especially as seen at its best among a people of democratic traditions and habits of mind, is a system of subjection to the will of the social organism, as expressed in an impersonal law. This difference between the system of status and the "constitutional system" expresses a large part of the meaning of the boasted free institutions of the English-speaking people. Here, subjection is not to the person of the public functionary, but to the powers vested in him. This has, of course, something of the ring of latter-day popular rhetoric, but it is after all felt to be true, not only speculatively, but in some measure also in practice.

The right of eminent domain and the power to tax, as interpreted under modern constitutional forms, indicate something of the direction of development of the political functions of society at a point where they touch the province of the industrial system. It is along the line indicated by these and kindred facts that the socialists are advancing; and it is along this line that the later developments made necessary by the exigencies of industry under modern conditions are also moving. The aim of the propagandists is to sink the industrial community in the political community; or perhaps better, to identify the two organizations; but always with insistence on the necessity of making the political organization, in some further developed form, the ruling and only one in the outcome. Distinctly, the system of contract is to be done away with; and equally distinctly, no system of status is to take its place.

All this is pretty vague, and of a negative character, but it would quickly pass the limits of legitimate inference from the accepted doctrines of the socialists if it should attempt to be anything more. It does not have much to say as to the practicability of any socialist scheme. As a matter of speculation, there seems to be an escape from the dilemma insisted on by Mr. Spencer. We may conceivably have nationalism without status and without contract. In theory, both principles are entirely obnoxious to that system. The practical question, as to whether modern society affords the materials out of which an industrial structure can be erected on a system different from either of these, is a problem of constructive social engineering which calls for a consideration of details far too comprehensive to be entered on here. Still, in view of the past course of development of character and institutions on the part of the people to which we belong, it is perhaps not extravagant to claim that no form of organization which should necessarily eventuate in a thorough-going system of status could endure among us. The inference from this proposition may be, either that a near approach to nationalization of industry would involve a régime of status, a bureaucracy, which would be unendurable, and which would therefore drive us back to the present system before it had been entirely abandoned; or that the nationalization would be achieved with such a measure of success, in conformity with the requirements of our type of character, as would make it preferable to what we had left behind. In either case the ground for alarm does not seem so serious as is sometimes imagined.

A reversion to the system of free competition, after it had been in large part discarded, would no doubt be a matter of great practical difficulty, and the experiment which should demonstrate the necessity of such a step might involve great waste and suffering, and might seriously retard the advance of the race toward something better than our present condition; but neither a permanent deterioration of human society, nor a huge catastrophe, is to be confidently counted on as the outcome of the movement toward nationalization, even if it should prove necessary for society to retrace its steps.

It is conceivable that the application of what may be called the "constitutional method" to the organization of industry—for that is essentially what the advocates of Nationalization demand—would result in a course of development analogous to what has taken place in the case of the political organization under modern constitutional forms. Modern constitutional government—the system of modern free institutions—is by no means an unqualified success, in the sense of securing to each the rights and immunities which in theory are guaranteed to him.

Our modern republics have hardly given us a foretaste of that political millennium whereof they proclaim the fruition. The average human nature is as yet by no means entirely fit for self-government according to the "constitutional method." Shortcomings are visible at every turn. These shortcomings are grave enough to furnish serious arguments against the practicability of our free institutions. On the continent of Europe the belief seems to be at present in the ascendant that man must yet, for a long time, remain under the tutelage of absolutism before he shall be fit to organize himself into an autonomous political body. The belief is not altogether irrational. Just how great must be the advance of society and just what must be the character of the advance, preliminary to its advantageously assuming the autonomous—republican—form of political organization, must be admitted to be an open question. Whether we, or any people, have yet reached the required stage of the advance is also questioned by many. But the partial success which has attended the movement in this direction, among the English-speaking people for example, goes very far towards proving that the point in the development of human character at which the constitutional method may be advantageously adopted in the political field, lies far this side the point at which human nature shall have become completely adapted for that method. That is to say, it does not seem necessary, as regards the functions of society which we are accustomed to call political, to be entirely ready for nationalization before entering upon it. How far the analogy of this will hold when applied to the industrial organization of society is difficult to say, but some significance the analogy must be admitted to possess.

Certainly, the fact that constitutional government—the nationalization of political functions—seems to have been a move in the right direction is not to be taken as proof of the advisability of forthwith nationalizing the industrial functions. At the same time this fact does afford ground for the claim that a movement in this direction may prove itself in some degree advantageous, even if it takes place at a stage in the development of human nature at which mankind is still far from being entirely fit for the duties which the new system shall impose. The question, therefore, is not whether we have reached the perfection of character which would be necessary in order to a perfect working of the scheme of nationalization of industry, but whether we have reached such a degree of development as would make an imperfect working of the scheme possible.

T. B. Veblen.

Ithaca.